CRUNCH
TIME

CRUNCH
TIME

**How to live a more ethical and
meaningful life without giving
up all your worldly goods,
joining a commune or losing
your sense of humour!**

MIKE HANLEY AND ADRIAN MONCK

ALLEN&UNWIN

First published in 2004

Copyright © Mike Hanley and Adrian Monck 2004

Allen & Unwin
83 Alexander Street
Crows Nest NSW 2065
Australia
Phone: (61 2) 8425 0100
Fax: (61 2) 9906 2218
Email: info@allenandunwin.com
Web: www.allenandunwin.com

National Library of Australia
Cataloguing-in-Publication entry:

A catalogue record for this book is available from the National Library

ISBN 1 74114 340 3

Typeset in 10.5/13 pt Caslon540 by Midland Typesetters, Maryborough, Vic
Printed by Griffin Press, Netley, South Australia

10 9 8 7 6 5 4 3 2 1

CONTENTS

Dedication

Mike says: 'This is for Claire, Max and Joel.'
Adrian says: 'This is for Linda, Ella and Ethan.'

Thankyous

Mike thanks readers Cameron Hay (who gave us the case study idea), Roebyem Heintz (who went out and bought a big SUV right after reading the Environment chapter . . . go figure . . .), Vicky Goldsmith and Dr Andrew Holden. And those who supported him professionally through all this: Gary Sullivan, Antoinette Breutel-O'Donoghue, Marilyn Dewji and Laura Dietrich. And not forgetting the literary ladies: Katie Haines, Lucy Luck (who wasn't), Elspeth Menzies, Tara Wynne, Jo Paul and Alexandra Nahlous.

Adrian thanks all those who balked at the crazy ideas, some who inspired them, and those who will inherit them, especially, and alphabetically: Mark Adams, Peter Bluff, Madeleine Creed, Gay Flashman, Steve Holt, Rupert and Sam McNeil, Gary Rogers, Benjamin Sykes and Kirsty Young.

INTRODUCTION

In the quirky and cliquey world of computer game designers, Sid Meier is a legend. He is one of the few men who can boost sales of a product simply by attaching his name to it, and he is famous for inventing the strategy game for the computer. In Meier's games, the player makes decisions and deploys resources in order to pursue a wider goal—for instance, managing and building a golf course in *Sid Meier's SimGolf*, or fighting the civil war in *Sid Meier's Gettysburg*. But his greatest invention is *Sid Meier's Civilization*, a sweeping, epic game that takes players from 3000 BC to the near future.

Starting as one humble hunter–gatherer, players amass entire armies, create cities, cultural communities, food supplies, trade links and diplomatic relationships with other civilisations, and discover technologies, engage in war, victory and defeat. It's pretty ambitious for a computer game, modelling, for the purposes of entertainment, the whole of human history and development. The game is now in its third incarnation, *Civilization III*, and has sold over four million units since it was first launched in 1990.

It's a popular game because, as Meier says, it 'provides a general sense of "history is cool and interesting" '. Players encounter historical landmarks and people that even high school dropouts have heard of: the Great Wall of China, the Egyptian pyramids, Julius Caesar, Abraham Lincoln.

Civilization works at a higher level too. You get to choose whether you want to be the Babylonians or the Zulus, the Americans or the Chinese, or whoever, and within that civilisation you are all-powerful; you can make all sorts of decisions: what transport links to create, whether to build an opera house or a grain store, whether to invade a neighbour or not. At the same time, everything you do has consequences—building an opera house is great if your people have a lot to eat and love opera, but a bit bloody stupid if they don't—so in reality your power is limited by the world around you. The same is true in the real world. There's no point in the President of the United States invading Iraq if doing so will alienate global public opinion and destroy existing diplomatic relationships—perhaps that's a bad example, but you get the idea. Nonetheless, the player of the game and the way they play it makes a real difference. You can choose to be a peace-loving civilisation or a warlike one—peaceful civilisations tend to spend a lot of time building cultural icons, and that wins them kudos across the globe; warlike civilisations, not surprisingly, spend a lot of time waging war—and the tone of the game will be dictated by that choice.

A *Civilization*-maker speaks . . .

What interested me was the way that the various forces that contribute to building a civilisation interact with each other. Diplomacy, cultural and economic strength, resources, technological progress, military strength and strategy, the natural environment, all these things combine in a great maelstrom that contributes to and takes away from human development. And this happens at both the level of the individual civilisation and with the progress of the human race as a whole . . .

Sid Meier, games designer
(in an interview with Adrian)

In attempting to encompass the whole of human development and experience, *Civilization* forces you to take a philosophical position on trade-offs and rewards, on fair play and just deserts. Luck plays a part, but in the main battles are won and lost, technologies discovered and cultures developed on the player's underlying strength and strategy. At the same time, both timing and the broader global scene play a part in the game.

There are three basic ways to end the game: conquer or be conquered in a Wagnerian *Götterdämmerung*; simply run out of time a couple of hundred years from now, or colonise the stars. In the tightly plotted world Meier put together, the end goals for humanity are pretty limited, but the decisions you make as a player, in combination with the natural laws that govern the game, determine which of these endings will come about. Real life, as we all know only too well, is neither so prescriptive, nor so easy. Pity, really.

Civilization players have the advantage of rulebooks and strategic advice. We, the players in the real human race, are neither so well briefed nor so easily judged. But there is an increasing sense that, for modern culture and society, and even for *Homo sapiens* as a species, we are facing critical decisions that could have a far greater impact than simply 'game over'. It is this feeling that motivated us to write this book.

Adrian works in London and Mike in Sydney. Despite the geographical inconvenience—an eleven-hour time difference for starters—we have a lot in common. Mostly we share regular things: young kids, both journalists, enjoy a drink, etc. But we also share a kind of niggling concern for the state of things; a nascent desire to figure out what the heck is going on in this crazy old world. More than that, we are curious about how to live a half-decent life in a world gone mad, both for our own sakes and for our kids who arrived on the scene and snapped us out of our youthful self-obsession. *Crunch Time* is the result of our investigations into these concerns.

I read the news today, oh boy

Terror, poverty, crime, environmental catastrophe, war, asylum seekers, greed, fraud, bankruptcy, pandemics, polemics—enough to put you off your cornflakes, really.

Apparently, says the news, we are the cause of the seventh (or is it the eighth?) great extinction—entire species are dying out in the thousands; dropping like flies, so to speak. Apparently, according to the papers, with cloning, genetic splicing, molecular engineering, neuroscience and stuff, we are heading into a 'post-human' future where the line between human, robot, computer and machine will blur ever fuzzier. Apparently, the think tanks think, in the decades to come there will be global water shortages, and we are going to be at each other's throats, literally, dying for a drink. It goes on and on. The wider world, it seems, is becoming an ever more terrifying place.

Meanwhile, on the home front, things aren't getting any easier. Families, communities, neighbourhoods are falling apart. Divorced, single-parented, blended, fragmented, whatever-you-want-to-call-it families proliferate; the old certainties—if they were ever there—are long gone. Then there are the kids—every life experience, from the birthday through to the rainy Sunday—who are the target of advertisers and marketeers. They're being raised in a world with so many choices—from the Wiggles through to Bob the Builder, from PlayStation through to Xbox—but so few meaningful ones; their days crowded with manufactured experiences and brand extension opportunities. If we adults are confused, how are the children supposed to learn positive human values, judge what's important and what's not, and learn the skills that are going to be needed to navigate this ever more demanding environment?

A job for life? Forget it. These days you can spend years of your life giving your all to an organisation only to find yourself surplus to requirements one random Thursday morning. We seem to be working harder and longer, maybe even earning more money, but the trade-off between life and cash is beginning to seem like a rather raw deal. We're told we are the engineers of our own careers, in charge of building, maintaining, training, negotiating, securing, styling and promoting the brand called 'me', but none of our bosses ever gave us a break on budget targets or project deadlines because we needed time for 'me'.

It's enough to make you wonder what is happening in our own great game of 'civilisation'.

And one more thing . . .

Late one night, after a few drinks, Mike called Adrian, who was just starting his day at work in London, and assaulted him with a stream of consciousness that sounded much like the paragraphs above. Understandably, for someone trying to get a job done, Adrian was a bit impatient with it all: 'Oh, what a load of moaning old bollocks,' he said.

'We've never had it so good. We're not starving, just the opposite—we're getting fatter every year. More of us than ever live in comfort, with all the mod cons. If the microwave breaks down, we buy a new one. The garage has two cars and a refrigerator just for beer. At the touch of a button we can get information, entertainment or education all delivered in the comfort of home or office from anywhere in the world, at standards that were inconceivable even a few years ago. We can travel on a whim to the world's great beauty spots or sporting events, and even if the job you left before you went away is no longer there when you get back, there will probably be another one along in just a minute.'

Adrian continued: 'Life expectancy is swiftly heading towards triple figures—and what a life. Standards of health and welfare are higher than even our parents could imagine. For the fortunate rump of humanity, the golden billion, this century offers medical breakthroughs that could see pain, suffering and illness pushed back into folk memories. What with cosmetic surgery, botox injections and the like, even the physical reminders of our mortality are capable of being removed, or at least disguised.

'So don't be so ridiculous, Mike. To sit there on the phone to me from 15 000 miles away in Australia surrounded by the abundant evidence of our progress and prosperity, to grumble at the state of things and to say we've got it hard is totally a load of shit.

'Yes, perhaps the newspapers today weren't brimful of great news,' he added, 'but they hardly compare to the stories of Hitler's crimes, Stalin's gulags, Pol Pot's year zero or the Great Depression's grinding dustbowl of unemployment and poverty. It would be hard to argue that baby boomers and below, born in the western hemisphere in the last half of the twentieth century, are not history's most favoured sons and daughters.'

He shut Mike up at least. But over the next few days even ebullient Adrian admitted that in his darker moments he also has that niggling feeling of foreboding; a dread that the game may be up and that things are going to change for the worse. This, we decided, is a crucial aspect of what we came to call *Crunch Time*, and it is all the more threatening for the fact that our everyday lives, lived in a world of abundance and impulse, have done so little to prepare us for its challenges and that the nature of the change is so unknown.

A few more phone calls later, we decided there are good arguments for saying the near future is going to be the most interesting route the rollercoaster ride of human history has ever taken. It will be interesting not just because it will be turbulent—when has human history been anything else?—but because there is a definite sense that as a species we are facing collective decisions that will prove critical to our future on this planet. Still, even if you don't believe the twenty-first century is more significant or important than any other period in history, there is one thing that undeniably sets it apart from other times: these times are *our* times, and it is our collective actions that will shape future history.

It is *our* news that appears in the papers and on television everyday—if we are living through the next great extinction then it is our problem, and our children's problem; if we are moving into a post-human future it is our humanity that will be transcended, or made obsolete; if global warming is happening it is our children and our children's children who will face the climate's changes. That is why we need to explore and understand these things, so we can make the choices that will give us the greatest chance of passing something worthwhile on to generations that follow.

This book is an investigation of *our* period of history—*Crunch Time*—the age upon which our ideas and actions will stamp their ephemeral mark. It is based on a radical idea—that our period of history is special; that we are going through a transition that is somehow important. The problem is that surely everyone who ever lived felt this way. But all around us there are signs that it *really is* different this time.

The start of the twenty-first century does not feel like a period of great optimism, vibrant cultural renewal, renaissance or rebirth. It feels like the best we can hope for is more of the same, and the worst we will face will be much, much more dire. Despite the wonders of our technology and the enormous leaps and bounds we have made in economic and social progress, it's almost as if the bad guys have won. Hippie millionaire John Lennon was wrong: we need a lot more than just love, we need low interest rates, missile defence systems, pre-emptive strikes on terrorist training camps, and detention camps for asylum seekers.

Meanwhile, those of us lucky enough to be born into the western middle classes have all our basic physical needs fulfilled and now we ought to be turning our attention to more worthwhile stuff—realising our dreams, understanding

ourselves and others, building better communities and futures
for ourselves, our families. In shrink-speak, the bottom of our
pyramid of needs is built and ready to hold all the better stuff
that is supposed to come on top. But for some reason that stuff
seems ever more distant, drowned out by the polyphonic ring
tones of our new mobile phones, hidden beneath the ever-
proliferating supplements of the Sunday papers.

Everywhere around us—Internet, fridges, cell phones,
newspaper supplements—are the visible signs of an ever more
sophisticated civilisation, but one that seems, nonetheless, to
be senselessly consuming itself. This book is an investigation
of that seeming paradox: the perverse nature of human civilisations, their relationships with each other and with the world
around them.

Crunch Time: Why now?

Doomsaying is hardly a new trend. A thousand years ago Archbishop Wulfstan in a sermon given in York admonished his
Viking-ravaged flock with the gloomy words: 'The world is in
a rush, and is getting close to its end'. Four hundred years
before that, someone higher up the ecclesiastical tree, Pope
Gregory I, surveyed the declining capital of the known world,
Rome, beset by invasions, floods, famine and plague, and
concluded that, yes, the world was swiftly drawing to a close.
Gregory's conviction that the world was fast coming to an end
was reached from a position at the summit of world affairs. He
was from a family more political than the Kennedys and served
his apprenticeship not just in scripture, but in running massive
estates, doing a little diplomacy and getting involved in defence
policy and the odd refugee crisis. Of course the world didn't
end, but the world Pope Gregory I lived in did.

Societies since then haven't stopped facing crises, and
feelings of foreboding as we look into the future haven't abated

at all. Still, this book's thesis is that, despite everything that has come before, we ain't seen nothin' yet. We believe that within our lifetimes it will be determined whether the human race can secure a permanent place at the universe's table, or whether our evolutionary chips are to be cashed in—it's now double or nothing.

If you were to bet on humankind seeing out the next fifty years, you might point to the many positive developments in human endeavour the twentieth century has provided: the unprecedented increase in affluence across Europe, North America and Asia with strong indications of more to come; the fall of totalitarian regimes across the globe; fast, cheap international travel; the plummeting cost of communications, telephone, Internet, television and the rest; rising education and literacy standards; great leaps of scientific understanding and the magnificent promise of discoveries in medicine and genetics; and the general resilience demonstrated by the human species when struck by both natural and self-created disasters. There are many reasons to think that the world in 2050 will, in almost every way, be a better place to be born into.

On the other hand, there are many reasons to believe that we won't be around to collect on the bet. Nuclear weapons may have grown old but they still pack a hell of a wallop, their ownership has multiplied, and they have been joined by new members of the WMD (weapons of mass destruction) family: cousins chemical and biological. Meanwhile, our numbers are set to rise by 50 per cent in the next fifty years—by 2050 some nine billion souls will press in on a world of scarcity. The scientific and technological progress we point to with such awe has a terrifying flip side: look at the ructions caused by genetically modified foods, cloning and the human genome project to name just three. The environment is a rich source of apocalyptic gloom, from global warming, threats to water supplies, increasing incidence of natural catastrophes, the disappearance of species and the destruction of rainforests, to local pollution and the environmental poisoning of large chunks of the population. Resources we rely on are running low. AIDS, malaria and tuberculosis and a host of other bacteria and viruses show at least as great a talent for survival as we do and new diseases such as SARS, as well as old ones like 'flu, threaten to create a plague that would hark back to the Black Death. Wars big and small proliferate. Meanwhile, the poor remain poor, the hungry remain malnourished and don't even ask about the meek. If you were of a pessimistic persuasion, you could argue strongly that we are our own worst enemy and our race is all but run.

Assume for a moment that there are two poles of reality for the future, that the collective decisions we make now in this great game of civilisation will directly influence the state of the world in, say, fifty years time. Say that there are two possible scenarios for 1 January 2050. For the first, imagine we get it right. On New Year's Day 2050, the sun will rise on a world where many billions of people enjoy lives of unfettered economic, social and political liberty; they pursue their dreams aided by whiz-bang technology the likes of which we have yet to even imagine; the environment is safeguarded by a combination of sustainable technology and the average life is long and balanced. On the other hand, imagine we get it wrong. In many ways, this is the easier picture to draw, assisted as we are every day by television and the newspapers: at dawn the sun will rise on a world that contains no people at all—the human race having extinguished itself or fled from the planet some years before. All that is left is a damaged web of life struggling to overcome the tears in its fabric caused by, and the cause of, the extinction of its most destructive species ever.

Is there a feeling of *déjà vu* here? Surely the same poles of possibility existed for anyone looking forward to the millennium in the middle of the last century? Then, the gloomy prognosis was of a Cold War threatening nuclear apocalypse, or else a world sunk in a long night of totalitarianism; while the cheerier outlook was to view the United States' post-war consumer boom as final delivery of the constitution's promise of 'the pursuit of happiness'. And what about Wulfstan? And Pope Gregory?

Perhaps people always think that their times are more critical than others, and it is part of the human ego to believe that our own part in historical development is more important than those that came before. In the end, the world in 2000 was a mixture of both ends of the spectrum and everything in between. This may be what is in store for us in 2050. Let's hope so.

How to read this book

What we aim to do is to look in turn at the big issues of the decades to come. Taken together and from a certain distance, we can see they have common threads which give us an indication of where we are headed, the forces that are pushing us that way and, most importantly, why. Exact conclusions are difficult to come by because certainty in this day and age is difficult to come by, but we do get there. This book is not a polemic, not a rigorous argument for any particular solution to any particular problem because, let's face it, rigorous belief systems, ranting polemics and concrete answers are *so* last millennium. But that doesn't mean we are left completely floating and rudderless.

Our answer to the confusion that reigns in the big picture is to disengage from the big ideas and to look closer to home, to our own lives and those of others who have been through confusing situations and come out the other side with something to show for it. We look at the big picture but try and bring it down to the local, to the things that we can change within our own lives and the lives of others. It means focusing on human characteristics that the twentieth century all too often forgot.

In 1966, in front of a crowd of students at Cape Town University in South Africa, JFK's brother, Bobby Kennedy, gave a speech focusing on the conditions that compel attention and action in every age, in every country and for every generation: oppression, social injustice, violence, danger and uncertainty. He was speaking out against apartheid in a country that would not repeal its racial laws for another thirty-one years. Nonetheless, his message was a simple one, and this book shares it: 'Few will have the greatness to bend history,' he said. 'But each of us can work to change a small portion of events, and in the total of all those acts will be written the history of this generation.'

Dr Seuss said it shorter in *The Lorax*:

Unless someone like you cares a whole awful lot,
Nothing is going to get better. It's not.

1
MONEY AND WORK

The Moncks came to visit the Hanleys in Sydney over Easter. We hadn't seen each other since the Hanleys left London a couple of years previous, and the kids had grown. There was much excitement as the visit approached: preparations were made and itineraries planned.

On the Tuesday after Easter Monday, we visited Sydney's famous Royal Easter Show. At one time rural agricultural shows were designed to display the best local produce (biggest pumpkin, fattest pig), but now these events—the ones in major cities at least—have grown into enormous consumption fests with sick-making rides, junk food galore and limitless opportunities to spend up big on everything and nothing. A trip to the show is a full day for the family, thrilling and exciting for the kids and murder on the wallet.

With three kids in tow—Max, Joel and Ella—conflict erupts almost every minute. The grown-ups are here to look at and enjoy the animals, the free shows and the wholesome entertainment on offer. The kids come to consume.

At the end of this exhausting and stressful outing we headed, as is custom, for the showbag hall. For first-time visitors Adrian and Linda Monck, the sight was gruesome and mildly shocking: stall after stall of plastic trinkets, candy and toys, packaged into themed ('Bananas in Pyjamas', 'Cheeses of France') plastic bags and sold for A$20 or more. All around, children and teenagers were laden with showbags full of garbage, each focused on their own orgy of consumption.

We escaped with only one bag per child.

Having staggered home, chased the children into bed and cracked a hard-earned bottle of wine, our day at the show became, for us, a metaphor for the *Crunch Time* world of money. For Claire Hanley, a recently converted environmentalist, the day was symptomatic of everything that is wrong with the way we live our lives today.

'Grotesque,' she called it. 'Wasteful, destructive and point-less.'

Linda picked up the remains of Ella's showbag and tipped the contents onto the coffee table.

'Eighteen dollars for this,' she said, picking up a ruler and poking at a plastic luggage tag, and then a ball-bearing puzzle. 'That's what we spend a month sponsoring a child in Malawi.'

'And we spent a whole lot more travelling halfway around the world for the frivolous purpose of seeing our buddies,' Adrian interrupted. 'It's all cash that could have gone to the world's starving kids. Showbags aren't evil, they're just cheesy.'

'They're bulking up the country's landfill with useless crap,' Claire retorted.

'And they're teaching *our* children that the consumption of pointless crap is a great way to spend the day,' added Mike.

'Well, we did have a great day,' said Adrian. 'And eighteen dollars for a "Bob the Builder" showbag is a small price to pay to put a smile on Ella's face.'

This is the conundrum of economic growth. We want the freedom to provide everything we desire for our families and ourselves, but having more materially makes us no better off emotionally. The more we have the more we want. We aren't any better off having bought all the crap from the Easter Show, but we feel it's impossible to deny our ourselves, let alone our dependants.

Too many toys

At the time of writing, between us we have three children, all under the age of five. And they all have too many toys. Huge mounds of un-biodegradable plastic that clutter up the corners of their rooms and beep and whistle when you touch them.

It is not that they have particularly indulgent parents, or relatives who work in toy stores—the *prima facie* evidence we have spied on parental excursions to other toddlers' bedrooms confirms that the toy oversupply at our houses is in no way an exception. Think about that. All over the developed world, from Kent to Kentucky to Kanagawa, there are middle-class children with too many toys. There is a toy glut. We are drowning in beeps and whistles, and it has yet to make the papers. And it doesn't take much imagination to stretch this metaphor from the toys in our kids' rooms to the toys in our own living rooms (plasma TV, multi-disc DVD, stereophonic broadband computer!), the class of vacation we take (Mauritius wreck diving, Club Med Phuket!) or the toys parked in the drive (all-wheel-drive, speedboat, ocean kayak!).

Like it or not, the success of capitalism has brought us, in the developed world, much to be grateful for. Between 1950 and 2000, the rich world grew by an average of 2.6 per cent a year, a rate that saw people get four times wealthier than they had been. Today most of us ought to want for practically nothing, really. Less than one per cent of houses in Australia and most of the rich world do not have a fridge; less then two per cent don't have a landline telephone; a house without a television is rarer than hens' teeth (in 1997 56 per cent had more than one) and 82 per cent have a VCR; just under 90 per cent of households have a car and almost half have more than one; in 2000 more than half of all homes had a personal computer, a third of which were connected to the Internet. Just fifty years ago these percentages for televisions and cars would have been almost reversed.

This kind of economic growth, which feeds directly into the number of showbags we can buy, the number of toys in our children's bedrooms and the number of cars in our garages, is a new innovation in the development of civilisation. For millennia—right up until the industrial revolution—whatever economic growth gave, population growth took away, keeping average living standards pretty much constant from the dawn of history.

Since the eighteenth century, though, countries have in turn taken on the economic structures of a modern state and taken off. The process began with the original Industrial Revolution in England, then the rest of Europe. By the end of the nineteenth century Germany and the United States had outstripped Britain's industrial production and the revolution reached as far as Japan. The rest of the world, sooner or later and to a greater or lesser extent, joined in the march to modernity—even the famously isolated mountain kingdom of Bhutan is now importing the marvels of satellite television and the stock market.

When countries start on the path to economic modernisation, miraculous things happen. Roads get paved, cars appear to drive on them, electricity is generated, peasants move from the fields to the cities which house and feed them (with variable success), phone networks get installed, illnesses are cured, TV sets pop up in households, showbags multiply and children's bedrooms fill up with toys. Whatever the downside for those of us drowning in excess, for those on the *real* downside economic growth *is* a wondrous thing.

Capitalism case study: Botswana

Take the quirky case of Botswana. Botswana is the size of France, but with barely a couple of million people. It is located within the world's poorest area—sub-Saharan Africa, an economic and general disaster zone. It also happens to be the country that has seen the *highest* sustained rate of economic growth per person in the *world*. In the last third of the twentieth century it grew faster than Singapore, the United States, anywhere.

A former colony, the British Empire didn't exactly leave it primed for growth. At independence in 1966, the country had one abattoir, a mile and a half of paved road, two schools and just enough university graduates to form a couple of soccer teams.

Despite these handicaps, the country has got richer at a blistering pace. Part of that is down to diamonds—they account for 40 per cent of the country's output. And a lot of this money has made the Botswanan rich even richer—Botswana is no egalitarian paradise.

Still, the money hasn't all disappeared into the casinos of Monte Carlo. The average Botswanan has done pretty well. Since the British quit the country, the adult literacy rate has doubled to nearly 70 per cent, primary and secondary education enrolments have rocketed and life expectancy has gone up by eighteen years. Economic growth has delivered a country where people live longer and are more educated, and the country as a whole is producing seven times as much stuff now than twenty years ago. Travel to Botswana and you will find a

---

The point of economic growth

Economic growth is essential for solving poverty. Without growth, there is little of the basics of life to go around—food, shelter—let alone too many toys. According to the World Bank:

- developing countries that grew fastest at the end of the twentieth century reduced poverty, infant mortality and illiteracy
- moderate-growth countries made much less progress
- low-growth countries actually saw poverty get worse.

stable and advancing country with educated and happy people. Look at their neighbours, such as Zimbabwe, and you witness the difference economic growth can make.

Botswana's problems are far from over, though. It has the highest rate of HIV infection in the world, at over a third of the population. But it can probably face the challenge better with a well-educated, literate population who are able to grasp catchy government slogans such as: 'Stay Alive, Condomise!' When the world's richest man, Bill Gates, was looking for the most promising place to put some of his squillions of excess funds, he chose Botswana, giving the country over $50 million in 2003 to fund an anti-retroviral drugs program. That money was matched by AIDS drug manufacturer Merck, providing both the drugs and the management of the program. Without the infrastructure and education enabled by Botswana's strong growth over the previous years, it is unlikely either of these investors would have been so enthusiastic.

For those who wish we'd never crawled out of the caves, Botswana shows that, in the twenty-first century at least, economic growth is a good thing. It is the only force we know of that can bring the billions of poor in the developing world out of miserable existences and into the kind of middle-class lifestyles and freedoms we wish for our own children.

So, growth is good. Hold that thought.

Poverty is the norm in our world

- of the 6.1 billion people on the earth at the turn of the century, 5 billion were living in poor countries
- of that 5 billion, over half live on less than US$2 a day
- of that half, 1.2 billion live on less than US$1 a day.

Tell these people economic growth is an unworthy goal—they might not think so.

How to get there

'Growth is good' might seem like a bit of a bald statement, but it is still the statement upon which most of our societies are built. Politicians get elected and tossed out on their ability or inability to promote growth; media pundits compete to shout the loudest about which policies and politicians do make the country grow faster; and countries rank themselves on their growth performance, boasting and chest beating when the numbers are good, or hanging their heads and searching their collective navels when they're not. Late-twentieth century history—with its epic struggle between capitalism and communism—has been dominated by the ideological battle about the best way to foster growth.

Most foundation economics courses begin with a professor standing at the chalkboard, declaring, 'Resources are scarce, and economics is all about how to exploit them in the best way.' Resources are unquestionably scarce—otherwise everybody's kids would have too many toys—but also unquestionably, resources are distributed in an inequitable way. Since economic growth became such a feature of developed and developing economies, economics—the 'dismal science'—has focused on how to get around this problem.

To date, two guiding principles have led economists' thinking, and those principles have laid the groundwork for the political systems of the world. The first was pioneered by Adam Smith, and the second by Karl Marx.

Smith v. Marx

Adam Smith argued that people enjoy their daily bread not because the baker is a kindly soul with a good heart, but because he is after a profit. According to Smith, society's best interests are served when people are allowed to get on with what they do best, and what will profit them most. Prices provide information about scarcity, and behaviour adjusts accordingly—the invisible hand of the market guides resources to those who can most profitably use them, or those who want them the most and are prepared to work to get them. In the end, as if by magic, social welfare is maximised. This is the foundation of the free-market ideology that guides liberal economies, such as the United States, Australia, the UK, Europe and everyone who wants to be like them.

Of course, there is much the invisible hand does not take into account, and the bulk of economic policy-making is concerned with dealing with the social problems the invisible hand doesn't touch. Think of the environment, poverty, the status of women, care for the sick, elderly and unemployed, education and other 'market failures'. But in the main, the message from Adam Smith is that if it ain't broke, don't fix it.

On the other hand, Karl Marx started with the premise that the whole of society is already broke—easy enough to agree with when you look around. Clearly, resources are not distributed evenly to start off with, and leaving it that way just makes the difference between rich and poor greater. It takes money to make money, as the old saying goes. Why should the baker benefit from his ability to bake bread and his ownership of the bakery just because he was born in a certain place at a certain time? Surely, society as a whole should benefit. The more uneven things become, thought Marx, the more social tension will bubble up. The solution for Marx was to place the ownership of the bakery and the baker's labour in the hands of the State, and then let the State decide where best these resources should be deployed. The result would be a more efficient use of the resources of the country, and a stronger shot at growth.

It was a nice thought but, as a thousand broken statues strewn across Eastern Europe confirm, it didn't work. It didn't work because Adam Smith's observation that the baker is innately selfish was right on the mark. Under State control the baker finds that he can buy the same amount of toys for his children no matter how many loaves of bread he bakes—so why bake a hundred in a day when he might as well bake half a dozen? What's more, the toy-maker draws the same conclusion. So even with his socialised wages burning a hole in his pocket, the baker can't find toys to buy. That's why queuing was considered a core skill in the old communist Eastern bloc—there just weren't enough goods to go around at any price, so it was first come first served.

The twentieth century settled this debate firmly on the side of Adam Smith and capitalism. Success in terms of economic power has flowed to the countries that adopted the principles of economic freedom—in other words, letting people get on with whatever it is they want to do with the resources available to them—within a framework of basic law and order. Some people say that Smith's victory has been so astounding that the fundamental economic problem of scarcity has been solved.

It is clearly not the end of the story, however, as many of the problems we face, staring down the barrel of the future, are the direct result of capitalism's extraordinary success and the 'market failures' that come with it. Some might say that capitalism has been too successful for its own good.

Why is capitalism eating itself?

If you can never be too rich (never mind too thin), how can capitalism go wrong? There are two reasons. The first will be dealt with more thoroughly in the next chapter, when we look at the challenges humanity faces preserving the environment that sustains it. It was most eloquently captured by Mahatma Gandhi (see box) and it fundamentally comes back to a question of limits—if we live in a world which is limited in its size, which clearly we do, and keep growing and growing, how can we avoid using all it has to offer?

A fundamental economic problem?

When India was on the brink of independence, a journalist asked
Mahatma Gandhi whether India would now follow the British pattern
of development. Gandhi replied:

> God forbid that India should ever take to industrialism
> after the manner of the West . . . It took Britain half the
> resources of the planet to achieve this prosperity. How
> many planets will a country like India require?

The second issue facing twenty-first century capitalism is
equally serious, but it is a structural fault within the system
itself. By necessity capitalism measures and rewards success—
for countries, communities and people—using only one
yardstick: money. True success, however, is more complex than
that. Or at least that's what we learnt at the London Business
School (LBS), where your authors met.

The Hogwarts of capitalism

LBS is an august establishment located in London's beautiful
Regents Park. It is dedicated to one thing: helping its students
get rich. Paradoxically it does this by charging them tens of
thousands of dollars in fees (in our case, close to A$100 000
each) to teach them how to squeeze money out of others. It's
a simple proposition for potential students: learn how to screw
others by being screwed yourself.

LBS is a kind of Hogwarts of finance. At the end of
the 1990s when we were there, the magic was provided by the
longest and strangest economic boom the modern world had
ever seen. Money was being magically made everywhere and
by everyone (except by people dumb enough to spend that

time studying instead of working), and it was being made in unusual and unprecedented ways: for instance, the dot.com boom was busy installing 27-year-old nerds in priceless mansions on the back of their ability to program Internet code.

The professors—wizards of the dark financial arts—were struggling to explain the phenomena. At the time, Dumbledore was played by Professor Gary Hamel. No long white beard, perhaps, but a rakish Errol Flynn moustache and wire-frame spectacles. Hamel was the epitome of the intercontinental business school hero: living in sunny California, teaching in rainy London, professing in the world's financial capitals, seen only in the biggest boardrooms of the world's business behemoths. Hamel had an explanation for the magic of business success in the 1990s. He spelled it out in *Leading the Revolution*, a colourful and breathlessly written tome published at the turn of the century. He discussed one company that embodied the principles that turned business lead into gold. Not widely known outside corporate circles, that company was called Enron.

> At Enron, failure—even of the type that ends up on the front page of the *Wall Street Journal*—doesn't necessarily sink a career.
> *International Herald Tribune*,
> 20 January 2003

> Controls form the cauldron in which Enron's innovative energies circulate. The heat comes from Enron's ambition . . . and from the chance individual dealmakers have for personal wealth accumulation.
> Gary Hamel, *Leading the Revolution*, 2000

Oops! Enron turns out to be the perfect example of capitalism's extraordinary single-mindedness. Less than a year after Hamel's book was published, Enron went belly up to the tune of over $100 billion—the world's largest ever bankruptcy. Gary Hamel was not alone in praising Enron. Before its collapse it was considered daring, unafraid, uniquely positioned to succeed amid the speed, risk and contagion of the business world of the time. Five years running, *Fortune* magazine named Enron 'most innovative company', and its Chief Financial Officer, Andrew Fastow (later sent down for ten years for accounting innovations of a different kind), won an innovation award from *CFO* magazine. No doubt Enron was an innovative company. It was just that its innovative talent was directed towards creating misleading accounts, persuading investors to hand over their cash, persuading its auditors to verify them, and concealing the real state of the company's finances. As Hamel put it in *Leading the Revolution*: 'The system focuses Enron's most ambitious and creative people on creating new wealth that drives the company's market capitalisation ever higher.' It just did it crookedly, that's all.

Enron claimed the retirement savings of tens of thousands of employees and the life of the company's vice-chairman (he committed suicide when he couldn't look himself in the mirror any more). Amazingly, despite a heap of connections with the Bush administration, the US presidency walked away from Enron untouched. It was just the biggest of a string of companies around the world that collapsed, taking down hundreds of billions of dollars. WorldCom and Tyco followed Enron in America; in Europe there was Ahold and Parmalat; SK Global in Asia; in Australia One-Tel and HIH. All of them achieved financial success by sucking in cash on a good story to investors. Some used sophisticated financing schemes, others engaged in old-fashioned double-dealing.

EPS I love you

The key to understanding the great post-boom accounting scandals of the early twentieth century is contained in Enron's 2000 annual report. The company, it announced, 'is laser focused on earnings per share'.

Earnings per share (EPS) is the number that tells you how

much profit each share of the company makes for investors. According to the analysts who decide which companies should get money and which should not, this number, or the growth in this number, is the single most important indicator of how well a company is doing.

Enron's pursuit of EPS growth persuaded its managers to create shadow subsidiary companies into which they could shove the company's rapidly rising debts, while keeping them away from the company's official accounts. Outright lying, in other words. As Enron's fictitious EPS kept skyrocketing, greedy banks and investors (only too willing to believe the stories about Enron's magic money machines) threw more and more money at it; the cheaper the money got, the more businesses Enron could buy, the bigger it got.

> To create man was a quaint and original idea, but to add the sheep was tautology.
>
> Mark Twain

But Enron's management recognised a crucial factor driving investment: performance and growth are rewarded disproportionately. This is a common conception—as we shall see in the 'Globalisation' chapter, it's a fact that our national leaders tend to rely upon a lot. If a corporation, or for that matter a country or a person, appears to be doing well, investors plunge money in, pushing expectations higher than future profits can deliver. When there's bad news, investors quickly bail—the proverbial rats quitting a sinking ship.

It's these problems, inflated by the acceleration, contagion and risk of our economic system, that raise critical questions about the way our economies operate, and whether they are fit to carry us forward into the future. The managers of Enron may have been lying about financial performance, but they were doing so for the benefit of their shareholders. One look at Enron's share price performance between the end of 1997 and the beginning of 2001 shows there were many who did indeed get rich on lies—provided they got out in time.

Unfortunately for Professor Hamel (and perhaps for Mike Hanley and Adrian Monck in the future), once you've gone to press there is no getting out in time. As Enron slipped spectacularly beneath the financial waves, Hamel, the evangelist for free markets and swashbuckling capitalism, changed his tone considerably. Suddenly his column in *Fortune* magazine was filled with concern for a 'starkly secular and ravenously materialistic' western society that has 'lost its spiritual capital'.

Perfection of means

For Mike, the story of Enron and the wave of corporate collapses that washed across the globe, and Gary Hamel's reaction to it, was proof that late-model capitalism and the way that growth, wealth, money and greed work together are out of whack. 'The focus on money and growth is all very well as far as it goes, but look at what happens when the growth disappears,' he said. 'Suddenly we have to find a new foundation for our lives . . . we find ourselves frantically searching for a new source of "spiritual capital".'

Growth is good, we agreed already—without it, our children are toyless. But the way we achieve it can be violent and hostile. More than that, a single-minded obsession with growth is as likely to be as ineffective as ignoring it completely. Economic growth is not the only kind of growth we experience in our lives, and isn't the only kind of growth that is good. In the boomtime of the 1960s Bobby Kennedy reminded economists that the numbers do:

> not include the beauty of our poetry or the strength of our marriages, the intelligence of our public debate or the integrity of our public officials. [They] measure neither our wit nor our courage; neither our wisdom nor our learning; neither our

compassion nor our devotion to our country; [they] measure everything, in short, except that which makes life worthwhile.

Kennedy would not have been surprised to see that GDP is not a good way to measure how well society is doing.

In response, Adrian replied that the problem is not so much with the system itself—the battle between Smith and Marx

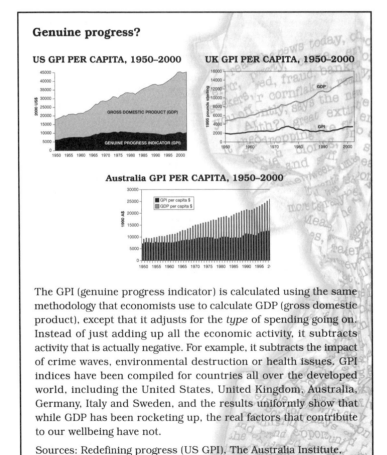

Genuine progress?

US GPI PER CAPITA, 1950–2000

UK GPI PER CAPITA, 1950–2000

Australia GPI PER CAPITA, 1950–2000

The GPI (genuine progress indicator) is calculated using the same methodology that economists use to calculate GDP (gross domestic product), except that it adjusts for the *type* of spending going on. Instead of just adding up all the economic activity, it subtracts activity that is actually negative. For example, it subtracts the impact of crime waves, environmental destruction or health issues. GPI indices have been compiled for countries all over the developed world, including the United States, United Kingdom, Australia, Germany, Italy and Sweden, and the results uniformly show that while GDP has been rocketing up, the real factors that contribute to our wellbeing have not.

Sources: Redefining progress (US GPI), The Australia Institute, The New Economics Foundation (UK GPI).

settled that one—but with the way people apply it to their own lives. Wily old physicist Albert Einstein put it this way: 'Perfection of means and confusion of ends seems to characterise our age.' The end is happiness, the means is money, but the two end up fused in our minds. We make more money, we consume more stuff, we buy more showbags, yet we still feel unfulfilled.

Appreciation of life, GDP and human development index (HDI): selected countries, early 1990s

Appreciation of life Ranking	Country	Average appreciation of life, early 1990s	GDP per capita (US$PPP)[a] 1994	HDI 1994
1	Netherlands	0.797	19 238	0.940
2	Iceland	0.793	20 556	0.942
3	Denmark	0.787	21 341	0.927
7	Australia	0.767	19 285	0.931
10	United Kingdom	0.760	18 260	0.931
11	United States	0.760	26 397	0.942
12	Norway	0.743	21 346	0.943
16	France	0.720	20 510	0.946
18	Philippines	0.693	2 681	0.672
20	Argentina	0.690	8 937	0.884
21	Canada	0.683	21 459	0.960
22	Germany	0.680	19 675	0.924
25	Japan	0.666	21 581	0.940
26	Italy	0.660	19 363	0.921
30	Nigeria	0.643	1 351	0.393
31	China	0.640	2 604	0.626
33	South Korea	0.620	10 656	0.890
36	India	0.603	1 348	0.446
43	Russia	0.510	4 828	0.792
46	Belarus	0.487	4 713	0.806
47	Bulgaria	0.433	4 533	0.780

[a] Exchange rates converted to US$ at purchasing power parity.
Sources: Chart from *Growth Fetish*, Appreciation of life—A. Wearing & B. Headey, 'Who Enjoys Life and Why? Measuring Subjective Well-being', in Richard Eckersley (ed.), *Measuring Progress: Is Life Getting Better?*, CSIRO Publishing, Collingwood; GDP and HDI–UNDP, Human Development Index <www.undp.org/hdro/98hdi.htm>

In reality, simply making more money, certainly on a national level, doesn't make us happier. There is plenty of evidence that shows that after we have achieved a certain level of subsistence—US$15 000 a year per head, according to the statisticians—further increases in GDP per head make little difference.

The evidence from surveys shows that in rich countries rising incomes do everything but make people more satisfied with their lot. On average, people in America, Europe and Japan are no more pleased with their lot than those living in the 1950s. In Britain, for instance, people are now almost three times better off materially than they were half a century ago, but overall well-being has hardly budged, in fact 60 per cent of Britons say they can't afford to buy everything they 'really need'. The same goes for the richest people in the richest country in the world. Juliet Schor in *The Overspent American* reports that 27 per cent of Americans who earn over US$100 000 say they can't afford to buy everything they really need. Pardon? In Japan, real GDP per person increased sixfold between 1958 and 1991, but the Japanese remained a miserable lot. In Australia, our incomes

---

Path to happiness

New Scientist magazine reports that the path to true happiness lies in:

- genetic propensity to happiness
- marriage
- friends who you value
- desiring less
- doing someone a good turn
- having faith (religious or not)
- not comparing your looks with others
- earning more money
- growing old gracefully
- not worrying if you're not a genius.

have increased by more than half in the past twenty years, but more than two out of three say they can't afford to buy everything they really need.

There is plenty of evidence to show that the correlation between money and happiness is very weak, or even negative. In Asia, for instance, the richest countries, such as Japan and Taiwan, have the most miserable people, while the Filipinos—without so much as a pot to, uh, spit in—consistently report themselves happier than any other culture. So getting richer doesn't automatically make you happier. Why not? One explanation is that people quickly get used to their new conditions—once you've got that inside toilet or that air conditioning or that DVD player, after a brief flush of happiness the satisfaction wears off. All these things were once considered luxuries, now they are considered essentials.

The other reason that people in richer countries aren't necessarily happier is because people's happiness doesn't depend on their own incomes, but actually on their incomes in relation to other people. Surveys routinely find that people would rather earn $30 000 in a society where $20 000 is the norm, than $40 000 in one where $50 000 is the average. You may be over the moon when your boss tells you about your bonus, until you find out that Bruce got a bigger one, at which point you get cross.[1]

It seems that keeping up with the Joneses is an all-important human driving force. Add to this our fear of losing what we've already got, and it is easy to see how we have created our own little prison of materialism. Like Prometheus, shackled to a boulder by Zeus and destined to have his liver pecked out daily by an angry eagle (he was immortal so his liver grew back each night), we find ourselves frantically redefining standards of success, achieving them, and then starting all over again.

[1] In one survey, for instance, students at Harvard University were asked whether they would prefer (a) $50 000 a year while others got half that, or (b) $100 000 a year while others got twice as much. A majority chose (a).

Our semi-criminal, semi-pathological propensities

Even economists didn't think it would turn out this way. Dismal science legend John Maynard Keynes wrote *Economic Possibilities for our Grandchildren* to brighten up the dreary days of the great depression. He forecast that humankind was well on its way to solving the fundamental economic question and predicted that three decades into the twenty-first century we would be eight times better off economically than in the gloomy 1930s. The long struggle to produce enough to meet basic needs would be over.

Well, we got eight times better off some time ago.

Keynes also predicted that economic success would mean we'd no longer have to slog our guts out to make a buck. Once the economic problem was solved, the great economist ventured, people would work for only about 15 hours or so a week. A few might work harder in the pursuit of wealth, but most would not, seeing the love of money as 'one of those semi-criminal, semi-pathological propensities'.

But what a semi-criminal, semi-pathological bunch we are. Even part-time workers struggle to do just 15 hours a week. The richer we are, the longer we work, it seems. As we have become richer over the past decades, we've found ourselves working longer and longer hours. Like a frog in a pot that doesn't notice how hot it is until the water boils, we often find ourselves at breaking point when it's too late. There is something extremely bizarre about this cycle—work harder, achieve more, become dissatisfied, work harder, achieve more . . . If insanity is defined as doing the same thing over and over again and expecting different results, then clearly we are all bonkers.

It may be human nature to be dissatisfied, but—like violence—it doesn't mean we have to accept it or celebrate it. Things do seem to be changing, though. More and more people are waking up to the futility of the rat race (even if you win, they say, you are still a rat) and dropping out. In Australia, a survey by Clive Hamilton at the Australia Institute found that 23 per cent of 30 to 60 year olds had decided at some time in their lives that they'd rather take a pay cut and change their lifestyle than stay on the relentless consumerist treadmill. The same results are showing up all over the rich world: in a similar survey in the United States, 19 per cent of the adult population said that in the previous five years they had voluntarily decided to make less money; polls in the United Kingdom show similar trends. Hamilton explains the results this way:

> The downshifters, often people with no more than average incomes, expressed a desire to do something more meaningful with their lives, and to achieve this aim they considered it necessary to consume less, work less and slow down.

Still, our increasing tendency to tune in and drop out notwithstanding, the majority of us are continuing to work harder, even as we have less and less real need to work. In the developed world, where we have provided for our basic needs many times over, it seems we get more meaning from our work than just the money we get in exchange for it—otherwise why would we work so damned hard? But herein lies the rub—if we work for the sake of working, why aren't we working towards something more valuable and lasting than simply filling our bank accounts and buying more toys? Perhaps that is the answer . . . or at least that was the conclusion we came to late one night in the business school bar.

The brand called 'screw you'

We were talking about branding—not cattle, but products. In particular how everything could be branded, even people.

'Tom Peters calls it "the brand called you",' Mike said.

'Tom Peters, the management guru?' Adrian raised an eyebrow.

'Yes. He says, "Today brands are everything". It's a "new brand world". Look at your clothes, you're branded; your car, branded; the school your kids go to, branded—branded, branded, branded. It's inescapable—Peters says we can't rely on corporations or organisations to manage our careers, instead we have to do it ourselves, to become brand managers of our own images and mould them into marketable commodities.'

'How depressing,' Adrian responds. 'Branding as therapy.'

'Well, if you take his message at face value, he is saying that in the new capitalist economy it's every man for himself, so we should stop looking at each other as people and start thinking of ourselves as the sum of our marketable characteristics.'

'It sounds even more depressing when you put it like that.'

'Not depressing. Good advice. Assume he's right, you are in charge of a brand called "you". No one else is going to sort your life and career out for you—it's up to you. This is the opposite of what high school and university taught us. We were encouraged to mould ourselves into what companies wanted, and then to entrust our satisfaction and lives to their goodwill. In the twenty-first century, what we know about making money starts with our own value first, then we make that value influential by using work to bolster it as we go along.'

'So my "brand values" don't actually have to fit in with what Tom Peters—or my company, my family, or the business school—might expect of me? They ought to be what I believe in rather than what others expect.'

'You got it.'

'So instead of the "brand called you", it could be the "brand called screw you".'

What does all this mean? It means that there is nothing wrong with being devoted to your work. But if you are going to dedicate your life to something, perhaps it should be to something more significant than improving the bottom line for some faceless set of corporate investors, or to meeting one pointless budget target after another. Perhaps it ought to be for something you will be able to sit back and think about with a satisfied smile when you're an old person reminiscing in your rocking chair, or for something you could tell your friends about with pride, rather than embarrassment.

Viva la revolucion!

Lord Kenneth Clark, a famous British art critic and father of womanising Tory politician Alan, produced a renowned television series called *Civilisation* in 1969. He characterised our own state of civilised development as 'heroic materialism'. At the end of the book that accompanied the series, he laments the emptiness of our culture of consumption:

> I said at the beginning that it is lack of confidence, more than anything else, that kills a civilisation. We can destroy ourselves by cynicism and disillusion, just as effectively as by bombs. Fifty years ago W.B. Yeats, who was more like a man of genius than anyone I have ever known, wrote a famous prophetic poem:
>
> > Things fall apart; the centre cannot hold;
> > Mere anarchy is loosed upon the world,
> > The blood-dimmed tide is loosed, and everywhere
> > The ceremony of innocence is drowned;
> > The best lack all conviction, while the worst
> > Are full of passionate intensity.
> >
> > > ['The Second Coming', 1920]
>
> Well, that was certainly true between the wars, and it damn nearly destroyed us. Is it true today? Not quite, because good people have convictions, rather too many of them. The trouble is that there is still no centre. The moral and intellectual failure of Marxism has left us with no alternative to heroic materialism, and that isn't enough. One may be optimistic, but one can't exactly be joyful at the prospect before us.

This feeling of desperation is clearly not exclusive to the twenty-first century. It is, however, all too easy when faced with the complexity of today's world to feel like the helpless victim, the dupe, the battler against a world filled with injustice and wrong, perhaps even more so than when Clark was writing all those years ago. Just dealing with the everyday stresses of getting to work and sorting out life, and actually recognising this feeling is in itself the first hint that it is time to stop; to wield the power we do have to change things. That change might be incremental, evolutionary even, but you could counter argue that we *are* a part of 'the system'—we have jobs and personal responsibilities. However, that membership gives us the right to dictate what our bigger goals are, where our pension money is invested, to what areas our society devotes its time and effort, the endeavours to which *we*, as card-carrying capitalists, wish to lend our support.

In the western world, we are lucky enough to be able to make choices. We need to work to put food on the table and

---

Some simple questions to help you identify the 'brand called screw you':

- What does your career stand for?
- Who is better off because of what you do every day?
- Do you believe in what you are doing?
- How ethical is the work you do—are you contributing to the next Enron, HIH or Halliburton?
- What is wealth in your life: money, security, friends, time, family, property?
- What is your wealth invested in: your home, a local business, the stock market, an ethical fund?
- Are you concerned about the big picture, the local, or neither?
- Are you working to change anything in your community for the better?
- What excuses do you use to avoid these questions?

to fulfil basic needs, but we do live in a surplus society. We can also work to build a better, more stable future for our children and ourselves. Making money has to be about more than being able to buy a warehouse full of toys. Surely it's also about giving our children something worthwhile and meaningful to weave into their own lives so that when those toys lose their lustre, they will have a set of values to draw upon.

As for us, Max, Joel and Ella won't be going to the Royal Easter Show again. We'll go for a picnic in the park instead.

2
ENVIRONMENT

'**H**olidays!' Adrian was back, and moaning. 'It was horrendous,' he said. 'We drove to a barn my parents rented in the middle of France. Four-year-old child, pregnant wife, seven hours spent in the blast-furnace heat of a non-air conditioned car.' (Europe was in the middle of the hottest summer on record, with thousands of people dying from heat-related ailments across the continent.) 'When we got there, it was 48[°C] in the shade, I kid you not, and 60 in the middle of the farmyard.'

'Jeez . . .' Mike replied. 'Hot.'

'We were sleeping up in the eaves, and it was like an oven. France was completely sold out of electric fans. On the last night we found a hotel with air conditioning. It had soft beds and swirly carpet, but it felt fantastic.'

'It's global warming,' said Mike. Then, thinking like an Australian, 'What's the water situation like?'

'It's fine. It chucked down all winter—torrential rain between October and March is the price for all this summer sunshine. But I tell you what, as we drove back in the heat and traffic, I said to Linda, "We're getting a new car, with air conditioning". And I'm ashamed to say I want one of those big four-wheel drives.'

'So you're going on at me about how damned hot it is and how the heat spoiled your holiday, but you want a huge bloody sports utility vehicle that spews carbon dioxide into the atmosphere and guzzles a tankful of gas just driving out of the yard. Hello. Join the dots, please.'

Not one to shirk a challenge, Adrian laid out his position:

- First, one hot summer does not equal global warming. In fact, apart from the rainy winter, it was a very pleasant change from the light drizzle that usually passes for summer in his part of the world.
- Second, even if the heatwave was a symptom of climate change, it is a long bow to draw between the travelling comfort of the Monck family and global warming. Many things may be contributing to climate change. Carbon emissions, yes, but also natural variations in climate, methane gases from cows' farts, and all sorts of other imponderables.
- Third, even if buying a bigger car with air conditioning contributes to global warming, it would be a tiny contribution compared to the personal benefits of riding around in a refrigerated Range Rover.

Mike had to admit Adrian was right. But at the same time, they both knew he was wrong.

The tragedy of the sports utility vehicle

The sports utility vehicles (SUV) plague is what economists call a 'tragedy of the commons' (see box). A tragedy of the commons occurs when a common good, such as a public park or fish stocks or the global atmosphere, is destroyed through overuse. Overuse occurs because each individual helping themselves to the good are only taking into account their own needs, and don't worry too much about what will happen if everybody else does the same thing. SUVs, as Adrian so aptly put it, are a great boon to personal transport. They are big and comfortable, and they make their owners feel safe and superior. But from the wider community's point of view they are a disaster.

SUVs might seem safer for those driving inside them, but they're not. They are difficult to manoeuvre, as the centre of gravity for SUVs is higher than a sedan, so they are prone to rolling. The demographic attracted to this particular type of vehicle (middle class, inner-city family drivers—Adrian hastens

---

The tragedy of the commons

Oxford mathematician William Forster Lloyd first wrote about the tragedy of the commons in the 1800s. He came up with a common formulation for the problem and it goes something like this:

> The local common, or pasture, is where anyone grazes their sheep for free. Because it's free, each shepherd tries to keep as many sheep as possible on the common. This works well enough for centuries because war, rustling and disease keep the numbers of man and beast below the carrying capacity of the land. Finally, however, stability arrives, and with it, the tragic logic of the commons.
>
> Each shepherd wants as big a flock as possible grazing on the common. But there are pros and cons to an individual shepherd sticking an extra sheep out to graze.
>
> *The pros:* as the shepherd pockets all the cash from selling an extra animal, the positive utility is almost plus one sheep for each extra sheep.
>
> *The cons:* after a point, one more sheep nibbling away at the common will cause overgrazing. Since the effects of overgrazing by this one sheep will then hit all the shepherds, the negative utility for an individual shepherd is just a fraction of minus one.
>
> So for one shepherd the loss is less than the gain. So, stick another sheep on the common! And another! And another! There is the tragedy. The pasture will become so overgrazed it will be destroyed. Everyone screws things up for everyone else.

to point out that the Moncks live in the country) so their accident rate is also higher than that of the average sedan. For everyone else on the road they are also a major hazard. SUV drivers can't see well out the back window due to their height, so stories of toddlers being run over by their own mums on their own driveways are a staple of tabloid newspapers. More than that, because the incidence of SUV ownership is on the increase, others on the road feel unsafe driving smaller cars, so pressure to buy into the SUV myth is intense.

As Mike also points out, SUVs are an environmental disaster. SUVs are far heavier than other passenger vehicles, so they require a correspondingly large amount of resources to create and destroy. They chew up gasoline faster and emit more pollutants than other vehicles. And because they are so big, and safety concerns are so strong, they boost consumer resistance to the development of smaller, lighter, potentially much more environmentally friendly vehicles.

SUV vehicles are a classic tragedy of the commons in today's world because owners of SUVs, who get all the benefits, don't incur all the costs. The costs are imposed on the wider community—the commons. We, the wider community, have no say in this because it is not, at the moment, recognised as a problem and the costs are not built into the price of the SUV.

This is just one example of the commons tragedies plaguing our world. We will all, in time, have to pay the environmental costs of the behaviour of all our society members—and the bill will be large. But before we get to that, we ought to put things in perspective.

Nothing new there then

One millennium ago, when the first Viking settlers steered their way into the fjords of Iceland, they were entering a virgin land. After seven brutal days on the North Atlantic, crammed into single-masted, square rigged, open ships (no cabins on the North Seas!), barely 60-foot long, the immigrants stumbled out onto an island that was a brand new natural idyll, still packed in God's box. They were greeted by uninhabited, pristine wilderness. Lush forests of birch, willow and alder stretched from the base of the island's volcanic mountains to its dark shoreline. The new country offered land and freedom. With neither kings nor lords to rule them, the Viking settlers made their own laws.

Six hundred miles from Norway, their homeland, the new Icelanders came prepared for self-sufficiency. They brought their households, their loved ones and their livestock. The only mammals living on the island were seals, arctic foxes and field mice. The Vikings brought cattle, sheep, pigs, goats, horses, cats and dogs with them.

The thing they needed most, and seemed to be plentiful, was timber to build ships, homesteads and fences, to burn in hearths and to provide charcoal for smelting bog-iron. The first arrivals felled the biggest trees. Successive settlers burned forests to create pasture when the grasslands were used up. As the population grew and the economy became more industrious and prosperous, over-eager herdsmen overstocked and overgrazed the now treeless valleys. With no system for conserving the island's forests, the amount and quality of timber the island could provide was quickly exhausted.

Like today's SUV owners, individual farmers weren't thinking about the greater good or the future of their people as they chopped and cleared. Barely a generation after settlement, Iceland's trees were gone. Good timber had to be imported, making longships too expensive to keep seaworthy. By the 1100s barely any Icelander owned an ocean-going boat, and that meant no travel. No travel meant no trade, and no deepwater fishing. Iceland, marooned in a vast, fertile ocean stocked with shoals of fish, schools of whales and alive with sea mammals, had become a nation of land-locked, subsistence farmers—

subsistence because without wood it was impossible to fence off grasslands to make hay to keep animals alive through the long, hard winters.

By destroying their forests, Iceland's Vikings lost the independence they'd sought. They became dependent on Norway for timber, trade and ships, and Iceland became a remote outpost, ruled for centuries by Norwegian kings. It's a history lesson to illustrate the value of environmental resources for our great game of *Civilisation*—economically, socially, politically, however you want to define it.

Icelanders aren't the only ones who messed things up by destroying the eco-system around them. The same thing happened on Easter Island and it's happened too in other closed environmental systems into which man has inserted himself.

Surely no modern land could repeat these dumb, destructive mistakes? Surely not somewhere as innovative, vibrant and resourceful as, say, Australia?

For 'timber' read 'salt'

Looking back through the fog of 1000 years to the Icelandic Vikings, it is still possible to imagine the sense of optimism in their hearts as they landed in their new country after seven days sailing across the northern seas. Not so the wretched First Fleeters who endured a horrendous seven-month journey across forbidding oceans, only to pitch up on a harsh and hostile continent. For them there was just the prospect of years of labour far from everything they had ever known. Still, human energy and ingenuity being what it is, many of the criminals who had been transported down-under turned their lives around and became respectable and well-off farmers, merchants and politicians, effectively duplicating the European lifestyles and social structures they had left behind. They weren't to know, of course, that by doing this they would lay the ground-work for the twenty-first century's equivalent of the Icelandic tragedy of the commons.

James Ruse, Australia's first farmer, was granted a dozen acres of land in Parramatta in 1789 (revolution year in France) while still serving time for breaking and entering. Stripping his land of native flora and fauna and planting grains and vegetables, he was paving the way for generations of pastoral-ists to do the same. Ruse, and his successors, had begun a process of fundamentally altering the ecological equilibrium of their new home.

Australia is the world's flattest, driest continent. Its native plants are thirsty. When it rains, they soak up pretty much all the water that falls from the sky. When a farmer clears the land and replaces bush and scrub with scrawny European plants, rainwater leaches through to the ground below, dissolving the vast amounts of salt that have lain as crystals in the soil since time immemorial. And there's not just a sprinkling of the stuff. Under each square metre of Western Australia's wheat-belt lurks up to 120 kilograms of salt.

'What's wrong with that,' you might ask, salt of the earth—biblical stuff. 'We all need a little salt.' Well we might, but the soil doesn't. As excess rainwater drains through the soil, it takes the salt with it. The more water goes down, the higher the water table rises—only this time it's a saltwater table. Salt-water destroys crops, rots buildings, rusts rails, ruins roads and costs millions. The technical term is 'dryland salinity' and it's one of the greatest challenges currently facing Australia's rural community, with more than 17 million hectares—an area twice the size of Tasmania—threatened by salt. It's another utterly predictable, utterly unforeseen tragedy of the commons—James Ruse enjoyed the benefits of his cleared farmland without paying for the costs of the dryland salinity that it created.

This is yet another tragedy of the thousands created by exactly the same cause: people. How on earth did we get here?

Out of the slime

About 400 generations and 10 000 years have passed since humans began cultivating crops and raising animals. There are many mysteries as to how exactly this came to pass and why, in fact, anyone bothered. Why was it that suddenly, after aeons of happy hunting and gathering, people decided to settle down and become farmers almost simultaneously in different places across the world? Was it environmental change—goodbye glaciers, hello horticulture? Unlikely. Was it that people suddenly thought it was sophisticated and clever to grow stuff and look after sheep and cows, rather than pick wild berries and hunt? Probably not. Theorists reckon it was something altogether different.

When a hapless young man suddenly finds himself in the family way, he is forced by social and economic pressures to settle down. And that is exactly what happened to *Homo sapiens* as a species. As we became more successful and our numbers began to grow, the regular, carefree existence we had lived as cave-dwelling hunters and gatherers just wasn't enough. The new, modern lifestyle of farming and husbanding animals allowed us to provide for our ever-increasing numbers. We still don't know if this was such a good thing, because the benefits of becoming a son of the soil aren't so clear-cut.

All the available evidence says that hunting and gathering makes for a pretty good existence. Even today in Africa, Kalahari bushmen (those not being driven to extinction by their government—the prosperous Botswanans) spend no more than two or three days a week finding food, while the Hadza people limit their hunting to just two hours a day, preferring to spend time gambling. Some anthropologists call hunter–gatherers the 'original affluent society'. *Financial Times* journalist Richard Donkin writes in *Blood, Sweat and Tears: The Evolution of Work* that progress, in this case from hunting and gathering to farming and settling, wasn't always forwards.

Hunter–gatherers have a wider range of foods at their disposal, therefore they face, arguably, a lower risk of famines. Their diet is more diverse and healthier, and generally they consider their way of life to be rather better than that of farmers or shepherds. If you think that farming was a natural progression on the long, slow, upward path of man, you would be wrong. Archaeologists distinguish the remains of the first farmers because they're shorter and weedier than their hunter–gatherer predecessors. There is little evidence too that agriculture is more efficient in terms of basic yield per hour of toil than foraging. But farming does feed people.

Chowing down on staple crops such as wheat or rice or maize day after day may make for a dull diet but those crops enabled us to feed more people. Growing populations need more food, and the only way to provide it is through farming. More farming needs more farmland, more farmland means digging irrigation channels and clearing forests, and so the cycle begins. Anthropologists call it the Neolithic Revolution. From our twenty-first century perch, we can see it for what it really was: the beginning of the rat race. Eventually it forced itself on pretty much everyone. As farmers, our days were more boring, more arduous, and our rewards less varied than when we had hunted. But there were too many of us to go back.

The next time you read in a newspaper that we are working harder and harder for less and less, take solace: it's hardly unprecedented. We might be working harder than we would as hunters and gatherers, but our ability to reproduce has increased rapidly—particularly in the last three hundred years. Meanwhile, we have built villages and towns and cities and produced artisans and poets and musicians and architects and all the good things that make up civilisation. It was the invention of agriculture that produced a surplus sufficient to provide for the priests, artists, politicians, scholars and so on whose activities are collectively thought of as 'civilisation'. In the

10 000 years since, the world's population has grown to over six billion people.

Still, it is not that long ago—about 400 generations—that we were actively employing evolutionary skills and mindsets that *Homo sapiens* no longer require. These behaviours include putting emotion before reason, confidence before realism, classifying others into 'us' and 'them', competition, contest and display. No longer wandering the savannah clad in animal skins, we nonetheless carry this baggage with us into the subway, to the office, to the opera, or onto a jumbo jet. We might dress up in dinner suits and communicate over mobile phones, but fundamentally we live our lives wired as hunter–gatherers.

As human beings we operate on psychological principles that discount future uncertainty by putting today over tomorrow at almost every opportunity. Celebrated economist John Maynard Keynes put it this way: 'In the long run, we're all dead'. This individual truism is, of course, a recipe for collective disaster.

The problems we are facing now are a direct result of the mismatch between our success and power over the world around us, and the world's ability to keep providing us with

---

Brain power

Our brains are hardwired to help us survive and reproduce in an ancient world. They do things like:

- make snap judgements based on our emotions
- take big risks when threatened and avoid risks when comfortable
- allow confidence to conquer realism and to get what we want
- create opportunities for display and competitive contest
- classify things and people, dividing groups into 'us' and 'them'
- practice gossip and mind reading as key survival tools.

Source: *Managing the Human Animal.*

The limits of the world we share were made graphically clear in 1969 when Apollo XI sent back the first photo of the blue planet—earth. The picture made millions of people realise for the first time that we all share the same ball. Environmentalists have won some important victories since then and some mad ones, but they have been waging a complex war against the entire way our societies are run.

hospitality. As four of the world's top scientists write in 'The Earth's Threatened Life-Support System: A Global Wake-Up Call', 'The Earth has entered the so-called Anthropocene—the geologic epoch in which humans are a significant and sometimes dominating environmental force. Geological records from the past indicate that never before has our planet experienced the current suite of simultaneous changes: we are sailing into planetary terra incognita.' In other words, we are guests in danger of overstaying our welcome.

Techies versus tree-huggers

One fact that seems clear to all concerned is that the natural world around us is changing radically and rapidly, and this change will only get faster. The changes will be the cause of much grievance and conflict, and they're intimately connected with the other issues discussed in this book: money and the markets, population and poverty, economic migration and the rest. Simply put, there are two approaches to the environmental crises that will emerge during our lifetimes, each put forcefully and often set against the other. Shrill rhetoric and a gulf of misunderstanding between the proponents of each makes them seem mutually exclusive and in desperate conflict with each other, but in actual fact they are complementary and interchangeable. Our only hope is the intelligent application of both when appropriate.

The first approach is that of the 'techies', with special appearances from the economists and the futurists. The techies feel that we have made an unbreakable pact with science and technology—since they got us into this mess they will have to get us out of it. This side of the debate thinks the only way to accommodate the burgeoning numbers of people on the planet and their material desires is to apply technology to solve the problems that development creates.

A couple of hundred years ago, British gloomster Thomas Malthus (we talk more about him in 'People, People, People . . .') predicted human population growth would outstrip our capacity to produce food. The global population was about one billion people, about a sixth of what it is now. Malthus, say the techies, was wrong, mostly because we now have pesticides, nitrogen-fixing fertilisers, and combine harvesters the size of apartment blocks to help us produce the food we need. We now husband over three billion cattle, sheep and goats, and apply scientific fishing techniques to drain the oceans. There are many hungry people in the world, but the problem is often not the ability to produce food, but the ability to get it into the mouths that need it. This is a remarkable achievement for mankind, and a point on the scoreboard for the technologists. In the same vein, the techies can point to a string of false prophecies that have come from the other camp.

In 1972, a ponderous group of European elder statesmen produced a doom-laden tome called *The Limits to Growth*. They reckoned humanity would soon run out of resources (see box). Their predictions were a little off the mark. Since the 1970s in fact, known reserves of all these things have increased, and prices have fallen. The techies reckon this is because human society is ingenious, and when resources become scarce, people find new ways to extract them, or switch to substitutes.

Techies view the future as a global game of whack-a-mole. Environmental crises pop up, only to be bashed on the head by the swift hammer of technology. Dryland salinity? A govern-

---

Predictions from *The Limits to Growth*, 1972

1981—only Bond villains are left smiling as gold supplies run out
1985—the temperature might be up but the mercury isn't moving—
  we've run out
1990—French café owners mourn the depletion of zinc
1992—there's no more gas to guzzle—petrol supplies are exhausted
1993—copper, lead and natural gas—all gone!

---

ment grant to a university department, some R&D in a corporate lab—science will solve the problem. Rising sea levels? Build bigger, better sea walls. And if a particular technological solution has its own side effects, intended or unintended, those too shall be dealt with in turn. This position is buttressed by the fact that the rich world has been getting relatively cleaner and has suffered less environmental destruction over the past 30 years, while the poor world has only got dirtier. Why? Because, they say, more economic growth means more technology, more money and more time to deal with environmental issues and, hence, a cleaner environment. Best encourage the poor world to catch up with us. Free trade and market forces, go, go, go.

Hang on just one minute, say the 'tree-huggers'. The problem is not too little development, but too much. Surely an ounce of prevention is worth a pound of cure? Our faith in science and technology as a cure for future woes is actually the cause of all our troubles. Yes, we can feed more people now than we could, but at what cost?

We spray our farmland with three million tonnes of pesticides a year (that's a sprinkling about half the weight of the Great Pyramid). We produce more nitrogen than the whole global total derived from natural processes. These things are poison. About two-thirds of the blue planet's fisheries are being trawled to destruction. The portion of the earth being farmed has grown to an area about the size of South America, and most of the pasture is grazed at or above capacity. We have lost about a fifth of the world's topsoil, a fifth of its agricultural land, and a third of its forests over the past half a century. We have changed the composition of the atmosphere profoundly. We've added to the carbon dioxide that is helping to heat the earth up, decimating habitats and native species around the world, and causing God knows what kind of problems further down the line.

Technology cannot save us from ourselves, say the tree-huggers. We need to save ourselves from ourselves, more than that, we need to save the natural world. Their vision of the world is one in which we awake from our technologically driven dream world, strap on our sandals and get back in touch with our true selves, living in harmony with nature and ultimately scaling down. Yes, fewer baths and all that kind of stuff.

Tree-huggers reckon that when we are living against 'nature' it is unsurprising that our violent lifestyle proves violent in return. For many hard-core huggers, the issue is not that the earth will bite back at human society—human society probably deserves it anyway—but the simple irreversibility of the loss of the environment. Once rainforests are gone, they're gone. Once a species is extinct, it is extinct—like Monte Python's Norwegian Blue parrot. *Kaput, finis.*

Tree-huggers take as their starting point that life on earth, human and non-human, has an intrinsic value in and of itself, that the existence or not of a particular species or wilderness is important because it's important, not because it necessarily provides man with something nice to look at, eat or to cure his ills. What this means is that the environment comes first, and humans have to play by nature's rules. These people reckon that the Icelandic Vikings deserved a good hiding from Mother Nature for putting their needs first. And they'll be there laughing when the last crop-duster crashes into the last computer. Cheerful stuff.

So are the techies and the tree-huggers poles apart? There is a movement trying to bring these two seemingly opposite opinions closer together. Step forward unlikely super-heroes, the economists!

One fundamental problem, say these optimists, is that decisions about production and consumption don't take into account environmental costs because prices don't reflect them. Remember the tragedy of the commons: Adrian's SUV? Environmentally aware economists are busy trying to come up with new taxes or incentives that will put a value on the environment, and give ownership of, and responsibility for, 'the commons' to all of us consumers. Meanwhile, politicians are busy trying to make sure that their constituents (that's us, too) don't have to pick up the tab. For tree-huggers the biggest and most objectionable problem is this—the very idea that we should value purely environmental goods, such as clean air and water, abundant fish stocks, or a species saved from extinction. Still, more important than whether we actually believe one way or another is the fact that our society is organised around economic principles that fail to take into account the environmental consequences of our choices. No matter what your intentions, if you want to achieve anything in the material world, it is extremely difficult to live an ecologically balanced lifestyle. Our everyday economic framework and our habits and behaviours mean that we live as if we were nothing more than an economic entity from birth until death, almost completely ignoring our impact on the wider world around us.

The original tree-hugger?

We destroy the beauty of the countryside because the unappropriated splendours of nature have non-economic value. We are capable of shutting off the sun and stars because they pay no dividend . . .

John Maynard Keynes, 1933

Back to the SUVs

Economists argue that we make environmental decisions by default every day. Unless we try and value the components of our decisions, we will simply be making poor, uninformed choices—like buying SUVs. This may be so, but even with the benefit of cutting edge environmental valuation techniques, we are still making poor uninformed choices, only now they have a veneer of scientific acceptability about them and they conform with the prevailing economic myth that drives so many of our decisions. Sometimes this makes them even more dangerous.

Take the high profile issue of global warming, for instance. It is fiercely complicated, both scientifically and economically, but the super-short version is as follows: Human activity (farming, forest clearing and industrial activity in particular) causes the emission of carbon dioxide and other 'greenhouse' gases—those that warm the atmosphere. There is no doubt that the amount of greenhouse gases in the atmosphere have increased over the past hundred years, and that human activity is the cause. This is uncontroversial. At the same time, the earth's climate has been warming, by about 0.6°C over the past century. This is also uncontroversial. The controversy comes in when making the causal link between the two: Human activity causes the earth's atmosphere to warm.

Some people reckon it could just be a coincidence, that factors other than man's emissions of greenhouse gases are causing the changes in the climate. Then there is a further step: warming will cause cataclysmic change. These two conclusions are questionable, controversial and very plausible. Here the teams wade in—the environmentalists versus the economists—each wearing their scientific boots. The Intergovernmental Panel on Climate Change (IPCC), a big group of climate scientists amassed by the United Nations in the late 1980s to look at these issues, is unambiguous. According to its 'Summary for

Policymakers 2001', 'Emissions of greenhouse gases and aerosols due to human activities continue to alter the atmosphere in ways that are expected to affect the climate', and 'there is new and stronger evidence that most of the warming observed over the last 50 years is attributable to human activities'. The second volume of the IPCC's report describes in over 800 pages the possible changes that will be caused by this human intervention, including increased incidents of storms, significant changes to the constitution of land and water resources, agriculture, forestry and fishing droughts, floods, rising sea levels, among others (see box). For the scientists there is little doubt that warming is happening, it is caused by human activities and the consequences will be serious. As a first and minor indication, in September 2003, when water restrictions were introduced in New South Wales, the Premier Bob Carr announced that it would be remembered as the first time global

---

Global warming bites

When we think of climate change, many people think of a slow and gradual process, but our knowledge of real-world climate change contradicts this. Fossil records show that generally when change comes, it comes quickly—hundreds or even thousands of years of steady state equilibrium, then an abrupt change, in as short a time as a decade. According to IPCC we can expect these problems within the next 30 years:

- chronic water shortages, putting immense pressures on water hungry agricultural crops and threatening lives in dry places
- rising ocean levels threatening coastal communities, particularly in poorer countries which don't have the money to build sea defences
- more tsunamis, storms and chronic flooding
- increased incidence of disease such as tropical viruses and bacteria.

Generally all sorts of chaotic and unpredictable stuff.

warming touched our lives (apparently he hadn't been with the Moncks on holidays).

How do the scientists know all this? They build hugely complex computer models that try to take into account the billion influences on the earth's atmosphere that combine to create our aggregate climate. The science is tentative, but it is the best we have, and over 500 scientists have signed up to the IPCC's interpretation of things. As we shall see in the 'Security' chapter, you and I, as mere mortals, should, as a general policy, be sceptical about all things. But some stuff we must take on trust.

The economists can't really argue about the science. But they can argue about what to do about it. Before we know what we should do about it, they say, we have to assess the costs. Here we enter the world of the really wobbly science, and a whole lot of politics, too. There are different approaches and different estimates, all produced by economists or scientists with competing agendas, funding sources and political approaches. In the end they come down to a fight between

---

Ten easy ways to cool global warming:

1 walk, cycle or use public transport
2 use compact fluorescent lights
3 buy energy efficient appliances
4 insulate your home
5 cut hot water consumption—wash clothes in cold water, fit a
   water efficient shower head
6 use solar or high-efficiency gas hot-water heaters
7 support renewable energy
8 service your car regularly and, if buying a new one, get a fuel
   efficient one
9 rate the energy efficiency of your new home design
10 plant, protect and conserve existing trees and shrubs.

Source: The Australian Greenhouse Office

Economist A who estimates (using the latest econometric modelling techniques, generously provided by Exxon) global warming will cost $X trillion dollars, and Economist B who says that A's methodology, respectfully, is bollocks, and global warming will cost seven times that much at least. They might as well shout: 'My daddy's bigger than yours'.

Meanwhile, forests continue to disappear, the size of SUVs sold in Tennessee moves smoothly from the sublime to the ridiculous, and the cultural heritage of historic Prague floats down the flooded Vltava river.

The sustainability mantra

The technologists and the environmentalists put themselves at the two poles of the spectrum. In the circles that discuss this sort of thing, however, the dominant philosophy of many sensibly meets in the middle. Pick up any environmental report from any international body (the UN, the World Bank, national and local governments, development bodies, you name it) in the past ten years, the one word that repeatedly rears its head is 'sustainability'—as in the 2002 Johannesburg Summit on Sustainable Development. Sustainability is a buzzword, for sure, with as many different meanings as it has mentions, but at its best it is where the techies and the tree-huggers meet and shake hands (with a fair degree of mutual suspicion, to be sure).

Sustainability means living a considered life—thinking about what we do rather than just doing it, and taking into account the discount rate we are levying on the future when we make our decisions. Sustainability means being answerable to the future. It means not taking so many fish from the sea that there will be none left tomorrow. It means that while we are searching for fuels that won't heat the global climate, we take it easy on car journeys, or pay extra for electricity that comes from windmills rather than coal-fired power stations. It means constructing government policy that redresses some of the destruction inflicted upon our natural surroundings by our violent economic system, by our rapid population growth, and by our general thoughtlessness. It means measuring the environmental damage we make in our everyday lives and figuring out ways to stop it. It means that if we are confronted by an environmental crisis we look beyond the immediate issue towards a way of ensuring the solution we implement doesn't cause greater problems tomorrow. It means changing our value system so that consumption of non-renewable resources is not cool. It means looking beyond today, using and polluting less and leaving some of what we've got for our children.

If the Icelandic Vikings had understood the concept of sustainability, the course of history may have been altered. If we don't come to grips with it, the consequences for humanity as a whole will be equally significant. In the end, the cause and effect of global warming and other environmental issues lie at our own feet. We cannot sit back as individuals and expect the scientists, politicians, economists or the press to sort it out for us—this simple exposition has shown that they haven't got a clue, or if they have a clue they are in a political situation which will not let them do anything about it, or they are downright wrong, or their motivations are self-serving. Whichever way you look at it, it is hopeless to rely on our systems of governance to sort out these huge systemic problems. And if these issues aren't to be sorted from the top down, then surely to live a good and aware life it is up to us to do what we can from the bottom up. It must come down to taking individual responsibility for moving the world in a sustainable direction. The only question is how.

Personal sustainability

Living a considered life means considering the impact of our own lives on others, today and in the future. In the 'Money' chapter, we quote how Gandhi observed that Britain 'took half the resources of the world to achieve this prosperity', leaving no room for India. His calculations were somewhat imprecise, perhaps, but the concept that there is a limited chunk of world that each person can consume before the planet's ability to renew itself becomes exhausted has developed somewhat since Gandhi spoke up. These days, scientists call this chunk the 'environmental footprint'. The idea is that each of us leaves a footprint on the world—going about our business everyday, consuming food, water, energy, housing and the rest—and that footprint can get bigger or smaller, in other words, use more or less resources going about our business, depending on how we live. People, cities or countries that live wastefully are not treading lightly upon the earth. They're doing something else on it.

Clearly, the actual calculation and measurement of footprints is completely shaky science (like corporate accounts), but the green group, the Earth Council, believes that with 6.3 billion people on the face of the planet, we each have 1.7 hectares to step on. At the beginning of the twenty-first century, the average footprint in developing nations was about 1 hectare. In the world as a whole it is 2.1 hectares, and in the United States, that apex of capitalist consumer culture, the figure is about 9.6 hectares. For every person in the world to reach present US levels of consumption with present levels of technology would require four more planet earths.

Ecological footprint calculations reveal other startling things:

- Tokyo's ecological footprint is 1.2 times the land area of Japan
- Sydney, occupying 0.7 million hectares, consumes over 26 million hectares of the country's resources
- the average American uses 9.7 hectares to support his or her current lifestyle—in comparison, the average Canadian

lives on a footprint 30 per cent smaller (6.9 hectares), and the average Italian 60 per cent smaller at 3.6 hectares.

The lesson from ecological footprints is not that, as Australians we each need to consume exactly 80 per cent less than we currently do (although that would be one way of sorting the problem). More it suggests that we each need to take the time to consider the way we live, and cut down on waste.

No doubt, environmental decisions and trade-offs are sometimes difficult to make, and the right answers aren't easy to determine. But the point here is that living an aware life at the turn of the twentieth century means thinking about what you do and why you do it, and making changes to your behaviour because you have to put the effort in—even if you are sometimes wrong. Nobody said it was going to be easy. As we saw in the 'Money' chapter, this applies to our work lives as well as our personal lives.

Some ideas for cutting down on your ecological footprint

- use reusable shopping bags
- print on both sides of your computer paper
- go vegetarian
- think about whether you actually need to fly in a plane—email perhaps
- buy locally grown and produced goods (one thing that drives Mike crazy is the fact that in Bondi you cannot get gherkins that come from anywhere closer than Macedonia—can't we pickle gherkins in New South Wales?)
- do you really need to buy more stuff—or are you consuming just to distract you from that horrid human condition?
- compost your waste
- take the time to think about your workplace, your industry, your company, your job—what can you do to make those things more sustainable?

Sustainable livelihoods

In *Good News for a Change*, popular Canadian broadcaster and scientist David Suzuki and his colleague Holly Dressel scoured the world for examples of enterprises and projects that were considered 'sustainable'. They found a bunch, from organic pig and chicken farmers through to Collins Pine, a forestry company that logs using only sustainable long-term forestry techniques. According to Suzuki, sustainable activities are based on three principles:

* they are generally local in nature
* they purposefully enforce low-income inequality within the organisational boundaries
* they are in it for the long, long term.

These principles are interesting because they grind in stark contrast to the principles upon which the industrial engines of the late twentieth and early twenty-first centuries are based. With their global focus, fat cat CEOs and quarterly reporting imperatives, the corporate monoliths that drive the economic growth that brings our children so many un-biodegradable toys are anything but sustainable. Ironic, isn't it. And worrying.

More worrying is that we perpetuate the system ourselves. We are the ones who shower our children with plastic toys, and simply fail to explain to them why constant yearning for material goods is damaging more than their own sense of self worth. If this vicious cycle is to be broken, it has to start with us.

It remains to be seen whether the techies or the tree-huggers will prevail. Instinct says that in the end, if we manage to squeeze through the bottleneck of the next few decades and into a more sustainable era, it will be through judicious application of both philosophies, using technological solutions where they are effective and safe, and using our connection to nature to control our irrational urge to destroy and consume unnecessarily.

It is ironic that the type of sustainable activity Suzuki is encouraging takes us back towards our prehistoric selves, when we were an integral part of the world into which we were born and were shaped and buffeted by the local forces of nature. It may not be the twenty-first century some science fiction writers had in mind, but for many it certainly seems less terrifying than being shaped and buffeted by forces from halfway across the globe. While we made that bargain all those years ago when we emerged from the forests and put fences around our goats, history has provided us with plenty of opportunity to learn from our experience. We are not land-grabbing barbarians, emerging voraciously from our longships any more.

The message is that in order to be answerable to the future you don't necessarily have to go barefoot everywhere, chain

Going to buy something new? Ask yourself:		
Do I need it?	❏ Yes	❏ No
Is there something I already have that will satisfy the need?	❏ Yes	❏ No
Can I buy it second hand/used/recycled?	❏ Yes	❏ No
Can I borrow or hire it?	❏ Yes	❏ No
What is the country of origin?	❏ Yes	❏ No
Was the product produced ethically (e.g. no sweatshops/animal testing)?	❏ Yes	❏ No
Is it of lasting quality compared to alternatives?	❏ Yes	❏ No
Is the product renewable in the short term (e.g. timber)?	❏ Yes	❏ No
Will it break down quickly in the environment (biodegradable chemicals)?	❏ Yes	❏ No
Is it organic or made with minimal pesticides/fertilisers?	❏ Yes	❏ No
Does it contain harmful or toxic chemicals or additives (colour, fragrance)?	❏ Yes	❏ No
Is it produced in an energy efficient manner?	❏ Yes	❏ No
Is it produced in a water efficient manner?	❏ Yes	❏ No
Will it be energy efficient during use?	❏ Yes	❏ No
Will it consume excessive water during use?	❏ Yes	❏ No
Does it have excess, unnecessary packaging?	❏ Yes	❏ No
Is the packaging reusable, returnable or recyclable?	❏ Yes	❏ No

yourself to trees and hurl yourself out of a dinghy against oil rigs in the North Sea. But you should at least be able to identify where your lifestyle and behaviour are inconsistent with your values, and work towards changing those things. Change the things at the margin first, but work towards being brave with your whole life—whatever that might mean for you. The journey into the future may not be smooth, even if you do compost your food waste. But at least you will know you did what you could.

The Moncks never did buy that SUV. Adrian says it was the money.

Ningaloo case study

Twelve hundred kilometres north of Perth on the North West Cape in Western Australia, the Ningaloo Reef is one of the world's last great marine wildernesses. It is home to a staggering variety of fish and marine life. Here, the world's largest fish, the whale shark, shares the waters with the bizarre snub-nosed dugong, about 500 species of reef fish, huge manta rays, and six of the world's seven species of marine turtle. Virtually unknown only two decades ago, scientists and others are scrambling to unravel Ningaloo's mysteries.

Bathed all year round in warm sunshine and far from anywhere, the 280 kilometre long reef is an increasing draw for tourists who are coming in greater numbers every year to search out solitude, swim in the balmy waters and snorkel with the unique wildlife. For the burgeoning eco-tourism industry, Ningaloo is a golden goose, a unique place where people can interact with pristine nature in a way that is becoming ever more rare in this increasingly crowded world. And people are prepared to pay for the privilege. It is an ideal place for tourist development—the question is, what sort?

In 1987 Coral Coast Marina Development, a Perth-based development company, had a plan: a marina resort with tourist and residential apartments, caravan and cabin sites, townhouses and timeshare buildings, restaurants, shops, boat ramps, golf courses and infrastructure needed for what was really a new town on the coast. In 1997 the Western Australian government rejected the plan as being too big and intrusive.

Three years later, the company came back with a more modest proposal, but one that had a fair bit of political momentum behind it. Environmentalists didn't like it, but the fact was that the government had invited the developers to come back with a more modest proposal and had given cabinet guidelines for the submission. To prevent the project getting approval was going to be a massive political mudfight.

'It was still the same beast,' says campaign coordinator Dennis Beros, 'and it had all the capacity to grow back to its original scale.'

What was most discouraging, he says, was that not only would the marina resort, as proposed, irreversibly damage the reef, it would close the door on an invaluable opportunity—the chance to develop a truly sustainable tourism infrastructure, one that would both protect the reef and give a permanent boost to the local economy and the people who live their lives there.

'The word "fragile" is bandied about a lot in the environmental world,' says Beros, 'but it only takes a minute in the air above Ningaloo Reef to see that it is just a ribbon of coral, eggshell thin, snaking its way 250 kilometres along the coast. Coral as fragile as it gets. A place where you could make few mistakes. We never advocated that there should be no development at Ningaloo. But it was clear that this development was going to kill the golden goose.'

For Beros and his colleagues at other environmental organisations, campaigning for the environment was simply what they did. Ningaloo was set to be just one of many campaigns, the outcomes of which are often disappointing. But there were early signs that this one might be different. A set of internationally acknowledged underwater cinematographers came in to see Beros at the Australian Marine Conservation Society, gave a donation and said, 'We must stop the development.'

'It was a wake-up call that there were other constituencies out there that were interested in this, other than the usual conservation suspects,' says Beros. And there were.

By using a canny combination of Internet communications, headache-inducing policy analysis, high profile spokespeople and public action, the team attracted interest, action and money from concerned people around the world. In July 2003, the Western Australian government announced it was to turn down the developer's application and seek to develop a program for sustainable tourism development in the region.

The Internet

The campaign's Internet site—which was featured on all campaign documents and 80 000 bumper stickers—included a link that enabled people to send a form letter to the Western Australian premier's office that put the argument for rejecting the development, and crucially allowed people to add their own comments. At one point the state IT office called the team and said it had just received 8000 letters.

'Please shut it down,' said the voice at the end of the line. The mail was generated from across the globe: about 40 per cent came from Western Australia, 30 per cent from the rest of Australia and 30 per cent internationally.

'It was timely for us,' says David Mackenzie of the Wilderness Society. 'Even now, spam issues would mean that we couldn't have the same impact. But, in parallel with the Internet activities, we were doing active lobbying, putting together real arguments, and developing a legal submission that in the end ran to over 100 pages of irrefutable scientific evidence for the resort to be halted.'

Audiovisual aids

The early interest and involvement of the underwater cinematographers gave the campaign a valuable boost by way of access to compelling underwater footage of the region. This both enticed news editors to run the story and instantaneously conveyed the values of the area to audiences. It also formed the basis of a short film for the campaign which was distributed via CD-ROM to state politicians and other decision-makers.

Getting the message across

Western Australian author Tim Winton became the celebrity face of the campaign, in the process attracting other celebs to the cause. Winton acted as 'blood in the water to attract sharks', says MacKenzie. 'He was a figurehead and he reached people who would not have even heard of Ningaloo—he attracted media attention at strategically important phases in the campaign when we really needed it.'

The campaign realised that it also needed a spokesperson who had their head around all the detail, someone who could mix it with sometimes hostile talkback radio 'shock-jocks' and front the cameras as the issue heated up. Paul Gamblin, someone far more accustomed to working behind the scenes as a policy analyst in government and now with the World Wildlife Fund Australia, took on the role.

Public actions and fundraising

The campaign organised one of the largest public rallies in Western Australia's history on 1 December 2002, attracting over 15 000 people to Fremantle. Many of these people dipped into their pockets to give the campaign $5 or $10.

Fundraising is a key part of any campaign because there are real costs associated with organising and managing a public battle. Gamblin puts it this way: 'The challenge is keeping a campaign alive when government obviously isn't going to fund it so you have to appeal to people who believe in what you're doing. It's almost like a voluntary tax—people will dig deep to support the common good. I think that says a lot. The great thing about these things is that a little goes such a long, long way because so much of it is fuelled by volunteer spirit and passion.'

The campaigners stress the importance of developing strong arguments and sticking to them: 'Play the ball, not the man,' says Gamblin. At the same time, it is important to draw on the body of knowledge available within the campaign group as a whole, to apply 'participatory democracy' wherever possible (for more about applying 'participatory democracy' see North Shore Against the War, page 115).

3
SCIENCE

Hundreds of thousands of words. Thousands of emails. Thousands of hours on the Internet. Hundreds of hours on the phone. The book you are reading is more than just print on page. It is the outcome of a dream we put together painstakingly over time and over distance.

Mike, sitting in his backyard shed in Bondi, spends the day researching some obscure subject on the Internet and on the telephone. Whatever comes together out of that is then sent as an electronic document seamlessly across the globe (we don't pretend to understand how) to Adrian, arriving at his desk in London's Grays Inn Road. From there, it is sent home to Kent, worked on and sent immediately and efficiently (well . . . sometimes) back to the shed in Bondi for Mike to pick up and work on in the morning, Sydney time. This book would have been all but impossible without the advent of technology. The same is true of literally billions of human endeavours across the globe today: modern life is defined, shaped and made possible by the magic that science has uncovered for us.

Look around—television, computers, drugs, cars, phones, planes, pacemakers, cameras, fridges—we are surrounded by the fruits of our own invention. The products of scientific and technological innovation frame our every waking moment. Call it what you will, the Internet era, the space age, post-industrial society, Crunch Time—we are living in an age of magic, and by most traditional measures are much better off for it.

Clark's view

Arthur C. Clark, one of the greatest science fiction writers ever, laid out his three laws of technology:

- When a distinguished but elderly scientist states that something is possible, he is almost certainly right. When he states that something is impossible, he is very probably wrong.
- The only way of discovering the limits of the possible is to venture a little way past them into the impossible.
- Any sufficiently advanced technology is indistinguishable from magic.

Still, rushing around from appointment to appointment, picking up text messages and popping our morning Zoloft, we wonder about how the balance of power between ourselves and the science we use to live our lives is changing. There's this niggling feeling that science and its fruits are conspiring against us, not-so-subtly trapping us in a cycle of invention and obsolescence, taking advantage of our human curiosity, needs and desires for some end we are not clever enough to see. Unstoppably, science itself chips ever closer to truths that we don't necessarily want to know.

Whether you like it or not, twenty-first century science and technology has a distinctly Crunch Time hue. It is handing us the tools of our own destruction, while providing people with a never-ending series of distractions to while away the hours before our extinction. Sound overdramatic? Read on.

How could they do it?

On 16 July 1945, J. Robert Oppenheimer stood on the edge of the New Mexico desert and watched the world's first atomic bomb unleash its fury. As his eyes filled with the light and rage his team had created, he muttered a line from a sacred Hindu text, the Bhagavad-Gita: 'I am become death, the shatterer of worlds.' Oppenheimer had led the Manhattan Project which produced the first nuclear weapons. It was science on a massive scale. About 50 000 people spent four years and over US$2 billion (in 1945 dollars) to hone the awesome destructive power of uranium. Looking back on that time, as the threat and consequences of the proliferation of nuclear weapons fill our newspapers and our nightmares, one question dominates: How on earth did these scientists—an extraordinarily moral and self-critical group—allow themselves to build the most destructive weapon in history? The question is worth considering because it runs to the heart of our understanding of the future of science and the direction and application of technology.

Many of the scientists had their own strong ethical views on the use of the bomb, but they carried little weight for the politicians and soldiers fighting the Second World War. The sheer horror that conventional weapons had wrought over the years of that war compromised countless moral arguments in the name of expediency. At first, objections to the bomb were based on its use against civilians. In 1939, a neutral America had warned both Britain and Germany against bombing cities, but by 1945 the bombing of civilians was routine. In March of that year more than three hundred US 'Superfortress' bombers conducted a massive incendiary raid on Tokyo. It razed 16 square miles (41.5 square kilometres) of the city and killed as many as 100 000 people. By contrast, the atomic bomb dropped on Hiroshima destroyed just five square miles (13 square kilometres) of the port. The 40 000 dead seems low against the Tokyo raid's calculus of destruction. War had already sacrificed morality for expediency by the time the first atomic bomb was ready. The only difference was that the concentration of power had changed—one bomber now did the work of hundreds.

The scale of the intellectual and technological challenge and the unfathomable complexity of the project allowed the scientists responsible for taking civilisation over the nuclear threshold to simply pass the buck. A simple compartmentalising of responsibility solved their ethical dilemmas. In a memo recommending the immediate use of the bomb on a civilian target in Japan, Oppenheimer wrote that scientists have 'no claim to special competence in solving the political, social, and military problems which are presented by the advent of atomic power'. This scientific hand washing, buried in a document intended for a readership only at the highest and most secretive echelons of the US administration, is important. This is the moment when modern science turns to us and says, 'You're on your own, kid.'

Three years later, after the Second World War has ended and the euphoria of discovery been spent, Oppenheimer reflected rather differently on his moral obligations. 'In some sort of crude sense which no vulgarity, no humour, no overstatement can quite extinguish', he wrote, 'the physicists have known sin; and this is a knowledge they cannot lose'. But sin is always original in science. Today's sinners are as high-minded, intelligent, self-deluding and obsessive as Oppenheimer and his team.

I have felt it myself. The glitter of nuclear weapons. It is irresistible if you come to them as a scientist. To feel it's there in your hands, to release this energy that fuels the stars, to let it do your bidding. To perform these miracles, to lift a million tons of rock into the sky. It is something that gives people an illusion of illimitable power, and it is, in some ways, responsible for all our troubles—this, what you might call technical arrogance, that overcomes people when they see what they can do with their minds.

Freeman Dyson
in *The Day After Trinity: J. Robert Oppenheimer and The Atomic Bomb*, directed by Jon Else, 1980.

In 1947, *The Bulletin of the Atomic Scientists*, founded by some of Oppenheimer's colleagues, began putting what it called the 'Doomsday Clock' on its cover. Ever since it has shown the scientists' estimate of the danger of complete nuclear destruction, reflecting changing international geo-politics. By the turn of the century, the hands on the clock had moved 17 times, swinging back and forth with the signing and breaking of non-proliferation agreements, outbreaks of war in different parts of the world, and the increasing and decreasing of tensions in various strategic theatres. On 27 February 2002, the clock was moved forwards by two minutes, from nine to seven minutes. This is the same setting that the clock had been placed at 55 years before, at the very beginning of the Cold War.

The threat of nuclear annihilation has remained with us throughout the last half century, but the passage of time has dulled our fear of 'the bomb'. Even the word sounds a little old-fashioned. But the scientific architects of our potential destruction are no longer limited to the world of nuclear physics. Different spectres of extinction have arisen in parallel. While mushroom clouds imply humanity's demise will come in one god-almighty bang, the kind of science that hits the headlines these days sees our decline more in terms of an evolutionary whimper.

New threats from science

Scientific knowledge grows exponentially. And that means discoveries and the technologies those discoveries create happen faster and faster. And that means potential threats emerge faster too. This exhibits itself in many ways. As just one example, take the growth in the ability of machines to compute stuff over the past 100 years. More than likely this ability will continue to grow equally, if not faster, for as far into the future as we can see. Technology buffs when discussing this growth refer a lot to something called 'Moore's Law on Integrated Circuits'.

Gordon Moore helped invent integrated circuits and started the chip-making giant, Intel. In 1965, six years before Intel rolled out its first microprocessor, Moore noted that the surface area of a transistor (as etched onto an integrated circuit) was being reduced by a half every year. Ten years later he revised this to every two years—which is, apparently, a better fit to the data. The chart below shows how the number of transistors of an integrated circuit has grown exponentially over the past 30 years.

It's not a law, just an observation, but it's worked up to now (to which the almost instantaneous obsolescence of your brand new PC will bear witness). Every couple of years we get twice as much circuitry running at twice the speed for the same price. This has been going on for as long as the computer has been

Moore's Law on Integrated Circuits in action

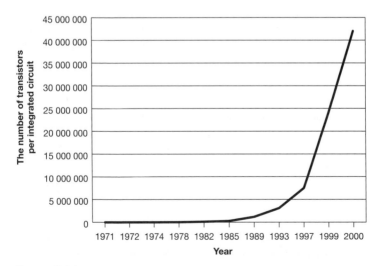

Source: Intel.

around, and the result is the wonderful devices we use today for everything from email or writing our last will and testament, to monitoring the state of shuttle launches and the productivity of toilet tissue factories.

Exponential growth in computing power has been going on for much longer than the integrated circuit has been around, though. Ray Kurzweil, a leading international expert on artificial intelligence and the inventor of the world's first print-to-speech reading machine for the blind, claims to have discovered the 'Exponential Law of Computing'. He tracked back to when the first-ever computing technology was used in the 1890 US census and charted it, through relay-based computers that cracked the Nazi's Enigma codes, to vacuum-tube computers of the 1950s, to the transistor machines of the 1960s, and to all of the generations of integrated circuits of the past four decades. 'Computers today,' says Kurzweil, 'are about one hundred million times more powerful for the same unit cost than they were a half a century ago.' This progress will continue, but some say that the limits of silicon will be reached within the next 20 years. Evidence and intuition suggest that something (nanotechnology, perhaps—see below) will enter to fill the void, and enable yet more improvements in computer processing to power indefinitely into the future. Exponential rather than arithmetic development means 20 000 years of computing 'progress' will be crammed into the next 100.

We all recognise the impact computers have had on our lives today, but what are its implications in the century ahead? While you consider this, remember the ability of machines to compute stuff is just one avenue of scientific endeavour. More computing power enables forward leaps in genetics, robotics, nanotechnology, even archaeology. Before we get too excited about a genetically purified, wire-free networked world, however, note that what terrifies some commentators is the way these technologies combine, multiply and reinvent themselves. Each one has the capability to outstrip the ability of governments, universities and even corporations to control them. The chief whistleblower on this was Bill Joy, formerly the top scientist at Sun Microsystems and an unlikely anti-technologist. He wrote a long and compelling article in techie magazine *Wired* outlining his own fears for the future of humanity, threatened by the power of the new sciences he and his colleagues were working in. The article was designed to kick-start the debate regarding the management and control of the twenty-first century technologies. It certainly did that.

GRIN and bear it:

The debate around technological development and its ability to outflank humanity's own evolutionary progress focuses on four particular technologies, known as GRIN—genetics, robotics, information and nanotechnology. These technologies are scary because they can all potentially self-replicate: 'A bomb is blown up only once,' says Joy, 'but one bot can become many, and quickly get out of control.'

Genetics: This is the study of heredity and inherited characteristics. Although the science of genes presents almost unlimited potential to aid in the treatment of disease and improve health, commentators worry that its potential to tinker with human nature will be open to abuse from our less noble traits: vanity, prejudice and the like. Worrier's alarms are set ringing by the very real possibility of genetically engineered plagues, viruses and the like which, when released into the population or the environment by malevolence or incompetence, will prove uncontrollable.

Robotics: The search for the ultimate robot demands a deep exploration of what it means to be intelligent and sentient, in fact what it means to be human itself. The ultimate fear is that by delving too deeply into the human condition we'll discover that in actual fact we are no more than a bunch of wires connected by electrical impulses—just a sophisticated robot. Some say that controlling sentient, self-replicating robots with super-human physical and mental powers will be beyond us.

(continues)

Information: As computing power and our ability to use it skyrockets, so does our dependence on the information held in the system. If your computer crashes that's it for your working day (remember the kerfuffle over the Y2K bug?). As society comes to depend on a network of incomprehensibly complicated databases and connections, so it becomes reliant on it working properly. So enters the bad guys or, more simply, complexity beyond our competence.

Nanotechnology: This science seeks to build objects at the molecular level, by arranging atoms in a particular way. Scientists envisage the ability to build everyday objects molecule by molecule by specifying the atomic characteristics of the object and sitting back while a nanotechnology machine goes to work. The out-of-control scenario envisages self-replicating, robotic, genetically engineered nano-replicators that begin to eat everything, consuming the world's atomic material and destroying all organic life.

Picking up where Joy left off, Martin Rees, Britain's Astronomer Royal, in his book *Our Final Hour: A Scientist's Warning* lists a cornucopia of catastrophes waiting to happen. On top of terrorism, smallpox and global warming, we now have to worry about microscopic self-replicating machines the size of molecules, reproducing out of control; lethally engineered super-pathogens creating unprecedented pandemics that wipe out great chunks of humankind; and particle accelerator experiments that create planet-destroying black holes.

Back in the 1940s, before lighting the fuse at Trinity, Robert Oppenheimer was worried that an atomic explosion might set fire to the atmosphere in an uncontrolled chain reaction. Oppenheimer was so troubled that he consulted his mentor, Arthur Compton, who suggested a risk–benefit calculation. He thought it would be better to lose the war with the Nazis than risk destroying the earth's atmosphere if that risk were greater than three in a million. Rees' estimate of the likelihood of science destroying mankind in the next 100 years is much greater: 'What happens here on Earth, in this century, could conceivably make the difference between a near eternity filled with ever more complex and subtle forms of life and one filled with nothing but base matter.' A 50:50 bet—how's that for Crunch Time.

But we might not end up in Rees's pieces. They are simply the latest gloomy contributions to a debate that has been see-sawing since the Manhattan Project gave us the ability to unleash self-inflicted planetary destruction. It just took an up-tick in volume and urgency as the twentieth century drew to a close.

Party like it's 1999

Put it down to pre-millennial tension if you like, but 1999 was a great year for the philosophy of science in popular culture. In that year Ray Kurzweil published *The Age of Spiritual Machines*. Another influential computer scientist Hans Moravec came out with *Robot: Mere Machine to Transcendent Mind*, which proclaimed that in the coming century our computational creations will outstrip us intellectually and spiritually. These two books illustrate perfectly the slightly weird and misanthropic tendency in computer scientists. The scenarios they paint suggest too much *Terminator*-watching. But they're also the imaginings of men who have a serious grasp of the possibilities of current technology and so demand serious consideration.

> At birth the infant will be clamped in front of the TV eye by means of a suitable supporting structure, and two sections of tubing will be connected to provide nourishment and to carry away the waste materials. From this time on, the subject will live an ideal vicarious life, scientifically selected for compatibility with the fixed influences of the inherited genes and chromosomes.
>
> Daniel Noble, Director of Research, Motorola in 1962

Kurzweil's and Moravec's ideas were eerily realised in *The Matrix*, a movie that came out in the same year. It was full of screen effects, sci-fi and martial arts, backed up by a blank-featured Keanu Reeves as a computer hacker given some startling news. Reeves's character, Neo, is told that contrary to the impression he is given by everything in the world around him, it is not 1999—it's actually a couple of hundred years later. The world as we know it has been destroyed in a war between us and the machines we created. We lost. But rather than destroying all the humans and turning to wind farms, the vindictive machines placed them in an orderly pod farm—an enormous bio-electric power plant—in which the bodies are nurtured from birth until death, as kind of human biological Duracell bunnies. But (in a bizarre moment of generosity) instead of keeping us comatose, they create a true-to-life world for our minds—the Matrix. It is an artificial world, as 'real' as the one we live in today, injected directly into our minds through a coaxial jack in the back of our heads. When Albert Einstein said, 'Reality is merely an illusion, albeit a very persistent one', *The Matrix* probably wasn't what he had in mind.

The Matrix—daft plot aside—translates a very Crunch Time human fear: that we may be superseded in the evolutionary race by the very devices we invented to assist us. Is this really possible? For Kurzweil, Moravec and their chums, it is not only possible, it's almost inevitable, and it is happening already—not in a *Matrix*-like confrontation between men and machines, but through stealth. Kurzweil even has a timeline.

To Ray Kurzweil, and thinkers like him, the redundancy of humanity doesn't seem unlikely or repugnant. Others see it as a foregone conclusion. Nick Bostrom, a philosopher at Oxford University, has published several papers that mathematically prove that the probability we are living in a Matrix-type computer simulation is much greater than the probability we're not. All you really need to do to come to this conclusion is assume that computing technology continues to progress at the exponential rate we have been seeing over the last decades, and that the human race doesn't meet extinction

The future according to Kurzweil

2009—A basic PC can perform a trillion calculations per second. High-speed wireless communication provides access to the web. Most routine business transactions (purchases, travel, reservations) take place between a human and a virtual personality, which often includes an animated visual presence that looks like a human face. Bioengineered treatments for cancer and heart disease have greatly reduced mortality. A neo-Luddite movement is growing.

2019—A basic PC can now equal the computational ability of the human brain. Computers are embedded everywhere—in walls, tables, chairs, desks, clothing, jewellery and bodies. 3-D virtual reality displays, embedded in glasses and contact lenses, as well as auditory 'lenses', replace mobile phones. Tiny nano-machines are beginning to be applied to manufacturing and process-control applications. Automated driving systems are installed on roads. People are beginning to have relationships with automated personalities and use them as companions, teachers and even lovers.

2029—A basic PC has the computing capacity of 1000 human brains. Permanent or removable brain implants are now used to provide inputs and outputs between humans and the global computing grid. Direct neural pathways have been perfected for high-bandwidth connection to the human brain. A range of neural implants is becoming available to enhance visual and auditory perception and interpretation, memory and reasoning. Humans now communicate and interact with machines more frequently than people.

2099—Kurzweil's geek-future ends when '. . . there is no longer any distinction between humans and computers . . . Most conscious entities do not have a permanent physical presence . . . Life expectancy is no longer a viable term in relation to human beings . . .'

(through, say, nuclear or environmental holocaust) before we reach the post-human future. His cheerful conviction that the future is bright, the future is robotic led him to found the Transhumanist Association (see box for their declaration).

The Transhumanist Declaration

1   Humanity will be radically changed by technology in the future. We foresee the feasibility of redesigning the human condition, including the inevitability of aging, limitations on human and artificial intellects, unchosen psychology, suffering and our confinement to the planet earth.

2   Systematic research should be put into understanding these coming developments and their long-term consequences.

3   Transhumanists think that by being generally open and embracing of new technology we have a better chance of turning it to our advantage than if we try to ban or prohibit it.

4   Transhumanists advocate the moral right for those who so wish to use technology to extend their mental and physical (including reproductive) capacities and to improve their control over their own lives.

5   In planning for the future, it is mandatory to take into account the prospect of dramatic progress in technological capabilities. It would be tragic if the potential benefits failed to materialise because of technophobia and unnecessary prohibitions. On the other hand, it would also be tragic if intelligent life went extinct because of some disaster or war involving advanced technologies.

6   We need to create forums where people can rationally debate what needs to be done, and a social order where responsible decisions can be implemented.

7   Transhumanism advocates the wellbeing of all sentience (whether in artificial intellects, humans, posthumans, or non-human animals) and encompasses many principles of modern humanism. Transhumanism does not support any particular party, politician or political platform.

Great chess players, lousy winners

Bostrom's boffins aside, there is real reason to be sceptical that computers will ever come close to being able to exist with anything near the richness of the dullest human life. Even the great milestone for the artificial intelligence boffins—the defeat of chess grand master Garry Kasparov by IBM computer Deep Blue—was something of a damp squib. When Kasparov was beaten IBM's share price soared. Geek philosophers loudly proclaimed the battle between human intelligence and machine intelligence had been won—by machines.

In case it was a lucky win, IBM dismantled Deep Blue the day after the match, scotching any chances of a human re-match. But IBM's chess monster was programmed, built and run by humans to play a very human game. Kasparov's response to the defeat was equally human: 'At least I have feelings about losing.' Kasparov went on to propose that chess be continued with players working with computers to augment the game. His response cuts to the chase. Chess is one of the ways that people fill their days. For some it's a living. But a game it is, and a game it will remain. Computers are unlikely to derive any satisfaction from pairing off to play a game of chess.

Machine 'intelligence'—even in the strictly defined world of chess—is not much more than that of a sophisticated pocket calculator. Deep Blue calculated 200 million positions per second, while Kasparov generally managed three or four. But the point here is, humans don't need more than three or four moves to see patterns, to look into the future, or to make judgement calls, good or bad. Deep Blue needed 200 million moves a second just to win a chess match. How many would it need to save a bad marriage, row a dinghy, or cross a busy street?

Five years after Kasparov lost, one of his pupils, Vladimir Kramnik, drew in an epic contest with a program called Deep Fritz. In fact he nearly won. Artificial intelligence experts admitted that Kramnik had played the more elegant chess, in other words, lessons had been learnt. When Kasparov faced Deep Blue he played the computer like a human adversary—selecting complex positions and trying to out-calculate his opponent. Deep Blue just out-crunched him. Kramnik, by contrast, dramatically simplified his matches with Deep Fritz by removing big pieces, like queens, in early forced swaps. Three games in to the eight and Kramnik led by two and a half points to a half. But the computer didn't tire and clawed its way back against an exhausted opponent, who blew the fifth game to end up drawing the series.

Chess is a rules-based game, and computers have changed it. When Garry Kasparov started learning the game he relied on books of openings. Now anyone learning chess can check out an online database of 2.7 million grandmaster games and statistics on the best moves. The game has become harder, but its qualities remain the same. And computers? In the words of the man who refereed the contest between Kramnik and Deep Fritz, himself an expert on artificial intelligence, computers remain 'pocket calculators'.

Dealing with Crunch Time science

So technology advances, wheedles its way into our lives, and we feel threatened and insecure, confused about where we are taking ourselves and where we are being led. The question is, what are we to do about these issues? Are they real or are they overblown, and what realistic action can we take to avert them?

In 1660, Blaise Pascal, the mathematician who invented probability theory, posed himself the question: 'God is or God is not—which way should we incline?' His answer was that we shouldn't look at the first part of the question—whether or not God exists—for that we cannot know. Instead, we must look at the second part of the question—how we should behave. In Pascal's mind, the consequences of behaving as if God did not exist (presumably drinking, carousing and generally doing bad things towards our brethren) and being proved wrong (roasting over the fires of hell forever) were so much worse than behaving as if God exists (living a good life, while passing up some amusing entertainment opportunities) and being proved wrong.

In a way, the same is true of today's science. Martin Rees's 50:50 assessment of our chances notwithstanding, we cannot know if mankind is laying the foundations for its own extinction, but we can behave as if that is the case. Even if we could dismiss the dark visions of doomsters such as Joy, Kurzweil, Moravec, Rees and the rest as science fiction fantasy, there are still strong reasons to be concerned about the spread of science and technology. The spectre of terrorists using weapons constructed from biotechnology, information or nuclear science; berserk nanobots wreaking havoc upon the world we live in; uncontrollable human created virus pandemics—these things are all real possibilities. What's more, each one of them presents such a vast downside risk (up to and including extinction) that even the most cautious observer would have to agree it would be wiser to, somehow, restrict and control the progress of science than to allow it to proceed unchecked.

The problem, as with all the issues in this book, is one of balance. The key difference between nuclear technology and much of the 'hi-tech' science being pursued today is that, in isolation, each of the GRIN technologies is being pursued for peaceful applications—to aid in the human struggle against disease and ageing, to expand our ability to build and create, to continue the never-ending push against the bounds of the human condition. But together they pose a real threat. Even though nuclear technology has since been used (albeit cynically and inefficiently) for energy creation and for medical research, the threats presented by nuclear weapons easily overshadow their peaceful use. Some say this is not true for the GRIN technologies.

While governments with big budgets and huge research facilities pursue nuclear technologies, less ambitious science is practised all around the world in different ways and with differing goals. Each individual advancement in genetics or robotics might be driven by the scientist's need to know, but together they hold out the promise of truly transforming civilisation. While they provide immense promise for many issues—poverty, hunger and disease—they also pose a threat. For the man who started this debate, Bill Joy, the answer is to 'just say no'. Scientists, says Joy, should give up pursuing technologies that could pose a danger to humankind. He reckons governments should ban the pursuit of potentially dangerous science, and impose a regime of inspection and verification. As an example of voluntary relinquishment, he cites the US's unilateral signing of conventions against biological and chemical weapons in 1972 and 1993 respectively. The challenge, says Joy, will be to apply the philosophy of relinquishment to technologies that are more commercial in application than military.

Joy is not alone in calling for caution across the scientific world. According to Martin Rees:

> The surest safeguard against a new danger would be to deny the world the basic science that underpins it . . . Should support be withdrawn from a line of 'pure' research, even if it is undeniably interesting, if there is reason to expect that the outcome will be misused? I think it should.

The threat of the new

From the violence of that salt . . . so horrible a sound is made by the bursting of a thing so small, no more than a bit or parchment containing it, that we find the ear assaulted by a noise exceeding the roar of strong thunder, and a flash brighter than the most brilliant lightning.

Roger Bacon, *De secretis operibus artis et naturæ*

Bacon was writing in the thirteenth century about some nasty new stuff that had crossed his desk—gunpowder.

Will relinquishment be possible? You must be kidding. There's unlikely to be any great global agreement on what is to be restricted and what is not—if one country decides to block scientific investigation into a particular area, others are only too happy to leap into the newly vacated space. Take stem cell research, for instance.

Stem cells are the building blocks from which we all grow. They develop to become foetuses, multiplying and changing into each of the separate parts that make up a human being. All the genetic information needed to create a whole person is contained within them. By growing stem cells in laboratories, scientists hope to find out all manner of things about human biology, growth and development, genetics, diseases and the like. Each step forward in stem cell research holds immense promise for medicine, and this attracts enormous public and corporate support. At the same time, opponents fear the implications of providing the power over life and death to scientists and their employers, and they point out genuine legal, religious and policy questions arising from experimentation on 'human' material.

While the Australian and US governments take a conservative view of the 'rights' of foetuses, Singapore and Britain actively promote biotech in all its forms, pouring government cash into research. Even today, the US suffers from a biotech brain drain as scientists in this area shift countries looking for more enticing research environments, or looser legal arrangements. Unless global agreement can be won on which technologies are safe to pursue and which are not, local bans on technology will be ineffective. Global agreement on this, as on anything at all, is one of the most elusive of *Crunch Time* aspirations. Besides, scientific progress does not happen in straight lines.

Newton's discovery of gravity didn't happen because of a government-funded program set up to drop apples on his head at regular intervals. It just happened. Funding plus research does not equal discovery. And the application of scientific advances is unpredictable. Take a recent discovery—bucky-balls. These tiny, football-shaped carbon molecules were discovered by accident off the back of other separately funded projects. But their discovery won a couple of chemists the Nobel prize and buckyballs—short for buckminsterfullerene—are now being considered in applications as diverse as AIDS cures and rocket fuel.

It is a vain hope to think that we can restrict progress through national regulation. Bill Joy's idea was to appeal to scientists themselves, saying that they should adopt an ethical code of practice, a Hippocratic oath of sorts, that would preclude them from pursuing potentially dangerous lines of inquiry. Scientists must be taught the importance of restraint and be empowered to blow the whistle on their colleagues when necessary. In his original *Wired* essay Joy wrote:

> This would answer the call—50 years after Hiroshima—by the Nobel laureate Hans Bethe, one of the most senior of the surviving members of the Manhattan Project, that all scientists 'cease and desist from work creating, developing, improving, and manufacturing nuclear weapons and other weapons of potential mass destruction'.

The sentiments are admirable, the problem is that relying on personal judgement just isn't good enough.

Many of the highly ethical scientists in New Mexico managed to convince themselves that atomic bombs were a necessary evil. The development of nuclear weaponry found sufficient new moral imperatives after 1945 to keep scientists' consciences clear enough—and this was in a liberal democracy. The same kinds of delicate moral choices weren't so easy to broach for scientists set to work in authoritarian states. How easy it must be for scientists to convince themselves that a particular technology is being pursued for good reasons, only to have their research subverted or re-purposed later by someone else? Personal morality, professional ethics—these are not unimportant things. But we know they can't be effective gatekeepers on the huge scientific population. An appeal to the individual scientific conscience may well pick off the odd doubter but, as an effective means of controlling the future path of knowledge, it's a non-starter.

So if national regulation and personal politics aren't enough, what about global institutions? Unlikely. Take for instance the International Atomic Energy Authority (IAEA). It was set up half a century ago by the UN to check the safety of nuclear reactors in member states, and to make sure they didn't use civilian power plants to kick-start nuclear weapons programs. But there are several new nuclear states today that seem to have gotten round the IAEA. And guess what? They're not in areas of the world renowned for stability and good neighbourliness. The IAEA doesn't have the power to go in and force countries to do what they said they'd do. When the US signed up for the 1972 biological weapons treaty the Soviet Union actually increased its research into anthrax and other bioweaponry.

There is no global police force empowered to check compliance with international agreements and penalise violators— and no such body is likely to appear in the immediate future. The closest we have is the United States of America, and many would say it is as much a part of the problem as the solution. The world's only remaining superpower resists attempts by any outside body to regulate its own affairs. As just one scientific example (never mind about global warming or international law), the US government opposes any strengthening of the international protocols against biological weapons on the grounds that letting international inspectors into their facilities would compromise not only America's security, but its 'competitive advantage' also. The answer, perhaps, may be to worry less about the technology itself and more about the health of the societies in which they are embedded.

For Dr James Hughes, a professor of public policy (and the secretary of the Transhumanist Association), the answer lies in the health of our democracies. He argues that only in a culture in which openness and transparency are fundamental principles can we be as sure as we can that dangers are being risk-managed. He sees Joy's call for relinquishment as a kind of Luddism—a 'misplaced attack on technologies that should more properly be directed at the unaccountable powers that deploy them'.

Hughes points out that in authoritarian states, people are not in a position to force regulatory agencies to do their jobs. This is true for science as for environmental, economic and other risks. Citizens of communist states were less able to protest about the spread of nuclear weapons, or shape policy, just as they weren't able to pressure the authorities to ensure correct safety standards at Chernobyl. As we will see in the next chapter, existing democracies also encounter problems when they become too dominated by particular groups, the military–industrial complex, for instance, or a corrupt class of politicians.

Another type of Luddite

The march of science might seem unstoppable, but the Unabomber thought a few well-placed munitions might convince scientists to down tools en masse. During a 17-year terror campaign of sending mail bombs he killed three technologists and injured many more. Why?

> The Industrial Revolution and its consequences have been a disaster for the human race.
>
> Line 1, Unabomber manifesto

The Unabomber was hoist by his own petard. The *New York Times* and *Washington Post* published his rambling 35 000-word manifesto after he said the killing would stop if they did. His brother recognised the style and shopped him to the FBI. Clearly it's going to take a bit more than a few parcel bombs to stop the onward march of science.

Hughes adds:

> the next necessary steps in preparing for apocalyptic technolo-
> gies is to ensure that all societies are open, guaranteeing the
> rights to investigate, organise and pressure for public health and
> safety, and that citizens are organised to counter corporate and
> military domination of the national and global state.

Rather than call for a halt in scientific progress, a call doomed
to failure, the solution is to strengthen civil society.

Overly optimistic, perhaps, but civil society, after all, is just
the sum of you, me and the rest of us, and our willingness to
engage.

What society has to do

It was the middle of that heatwave in the UK, and Adrian was
sweltering in 30°C heat on the lawn in Kent. Mike, in Bondi,
huddled in his shed on a cool winter's night. The telephone,
however, was running hot.

'You don't actually believe all this rubbish, do you?' Adrian
was saying. 'About robots gone mad and genetically engineered
plagues let loose on an unsuspecting population? It's all a bit
Saturday night at the movies.'

There was a long pause at the end of the line.

'It doesn't really matter if I believe it or not,' came the
response. 'What matters is that I'm not really in a position to
understand whether it's a possibility, or even to know that there
is somebody out there whose job it is to know whether it's a
possibility or not. It comes down to the fact that I feel helpless
against greater forces. I don't feel like I have a say in the future,
and I feel like I should.'

Adrian replied that people have never had a say in the
future. 'That is not what life is about,' he said. 'When people
felt helpless in years gone by, we prayed: in fact we still do.

Societies used to bend their efforts to building ever greater churches and cathedrals and temples to future-proof them against all the nasty things that might happen. But that isn't enough for us any more, now we want to know that every risk we take is assessed and managed and controlled. If something goes wrong we need to blame somebody in particular, some regulatory body for not doing its job, or some politician for not implementing the right policy. Perhaps it was just easier when we could turn around and say we should have sacrificed a few more chickens.'

Mike sighed. 'Like you said, the point is that it's not enough for us these days.'

So what would be enough? The point of this science chapter, we decided, is not to scare people witless about the terrors that technology will inevitably bring, or to get them out onto the streets with placards reading, 'Down with nano-tech' or 'Stem cell research kills babies'. It is to ensure we all understand the risks and rewards of scientific progress, and that it is possible to control and manage those risks, but only within the confines of a healthy society where people are informed and care.

We need communities that are comfortable talking about the real issues—that aren't dominated by special interest groups, or by the overly conservative or the overly libertarian. It's crucial that twenty-first century societies are able to make decisions based on reasonably informed and rational principles backed up by dollops of human instinct, and by citizens who understand the issues, care about them, and are empowered to participate in the debate and shape its outcome. It is only if we fail in this that the more gruesome sci-fi spectres may come to pass.

It's unlikely there will ever be a global authority to protect us from weird science. Once again, the issue is laid at our door. For that reason it is essential we understand the issues that scientific progress presents us, and be prepared to act. The task is big, but it is far from hopeless. It is not necessary to be an astrophysicist or a biochemist to understand the issues behind scientific research. You don't have to understand science to understand it is wrong that 90 per cent of the US$70 billion spent on health research worldwide is devoted to diseases that account for less than 10 per cent of the global disease burden, such as cures for male pattern baldness, acne and other 'diseases' of the rich.

Science has given us access to information and tools to make ourselves heard. A surf on the Internet to gather information on potential diagnoses often precedes a visit to the doctor. Lobbying by ethical groups is organised by email and mobile phone. The fundamentals, however, are energy and engagement. *Time* magazine's 'Person of the Twentieth Century' may have said it best:

> A human being is part of a whole called by us the 'Universe', a part limited in time and space. He experiences himself, his thoughts and feelings, as something separated from the rest—a kind of optical delusion of his consciousness. This delusion is a kind of prison for us, restricting us to our personal desires and to affection for a few persons nearest us. Our task must be to free ourselves from this prison by widening our circles of compassion to embrace all living creatures and the whole of nature in its beauty.

Even Einstein could come over all mushy when the occasion demanded. For Einstein, science was a flight from the *I* and the *we* to the *it*. But the only way forward, he thought, was to take the journey back from the *it* to the *we* and the *I*.

More than half a century has passed since Oppenheimer and his team invented the nuclear bomb. It hasn't always been comfortable or secure (and we still might be just seven minutes from midnight) but so far we've managed not to blow ourselves into kingdom come. Eternity is a long time, but we started it back in New Mexico.

Technology has brought us revolutions before. In one earlier technological wave of change, a new world was opened where people could immerse themselves in a form of com-munication that broke the verbal and physical world of human contact. A world where voices in your head replaced the spoken word and people became able to immerse themselves in a brave new world of ideas, imagination and knowledge. The technol-ogy was print, and the information revolution of the sixteenth century was the book. Literature did change the world. They burned books in the middle of Florence more than half a millennium ago (they still burn them today in other places in the world), but books have not yet brought about the downfall of humankind. Maybe just give them a little more time.

4
DEMOCRACY

————Original message————
From: Mike Hanley
Sent: Friday, 14 February 2003 9:31 PM
To: Adrian Monck
Subject: You around tomorrow for a chat?

————Original message————
From: Adrian Monck
To: Mike Hanley
Sent: Friday, 14 February 2003 10:45 AM
Subject: I'm in the newsroom doing a shift tomorrow—monthly weekend work.

————Original message————
From: Mike Hanley
Sent: Saturday, 15 February 2003 11:45 PM
To: Adrian Monck
Subject: Demos
Watching the London Iraq demos on telly. We went today in Sydney—it was amazing. Crowded and hot, but there was a real feeling. I've never seen so many people clearly passionate about something political.

————Original message————
From: Adrian Monck
Sent: Saturday, 15 February 2003 12:48 AM
To: Mike Hanley
Subject: Re: Demos
They're estimating over a million people here. And it looks that way from what I can see—we've got five reporters downtown and every shot is packed.
Got footage coming in from across Europe—Spain, Italy, France, Germany, even the Russians are out. It looks bloody freezing.

————Original message————
From: Mike Hanley
To: Adrian Monck
Sent: Saturday, 15 February 2003 11:51 PM
Subject: Re: Re: Demos
It's brilliant. What is this if it isn't *Crunch Time* democracy?

————Original message————
From: Adrian Monck
To: Mike Hanley
Sent: Saturday, 15 February 2003 12:55 AM
Subject: Re: Re: Re: Demos
It's a waste of time, that's what it is.

A waste of time! Over five million people in Australia, the UK, and the US (to name only the countries in the 'coalition of the willing') turned out on the streets that day to shout at their governments about the impending war on Iraq. And they were wasting their time. As Adrian pointed out on the email that day, democratically elected leaders listen to the people when it suits them. When it doesn't, they play the representative democracy card: 'You elected us to make decisions for you, now let us make

Anti-war protests (estimated figures)

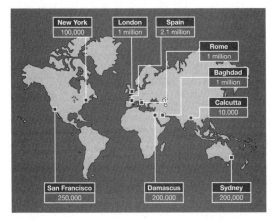

Source: BBC Online.

them.' Always one to make his point forcefully (if somewhat pretentiously) Adrian concluded the exchange with a quote:

> The individual man does not have opinions on all public affairs . . . He does not know what is happening, why it is happening, what ought to happen. I cannot imagine how he could know, and there is not the least reason for thinking, as mystical democrats have thought, that the compounding of individual ignorances in masses of people can produce a continuous directing force in public affairs.

American journalist Walter Lippman wrote that back in 1925. The powerful whiff of cynicism still rises from each sentence like smoke from a Senator's Gran Corona. Born at the end of the 1880s, Lippman started life a socialist. But by the 1920s he'd come to the conclusion that the modern world was just too complex and people just too dumb—not only for socialism, but for democracy.

It wasn't just getting older and grumpier that changed his mind. Lippman's cynicism was triggered doing patriotic work

> **demagogue** /demmagog/ *n.* (US –gog) **1** a political agitator
> appealing to the basest instincts of a mob. **2** *hist.* a leader
> of the people esp. in ancient times
>
> *Oxford English Dictionary and Thesaurus*

for President Woodrow Wilson, getting his fellow Americans excited about joining the First World War. Serving on the presidential propaganda committee impressed upon Lippman that democracy was not about rational debate producing reasonable policies. It was all about policy-makers' realities and public perception of them.

He had realised what democrats in ancient Greece knew only too well—that people's better judgement could be swayed more easily by emotion than by reason. The Greeks called it demagoguery, the Victorians called it rabble-rousing, and it could, on occasion, get you kicked out of town. One of Lippman's fellow propagandists, Edward Bernays, coined a modern, less awkward term for it: public relations.

Success in kicking the Kaiser and selling the First World War to the American public didn't give Lippman a warm fuzzy feeling. Like a comedian who hates his audiences for laughing at cheap gags, Lippman came to despise the 'bewildered herd' he'd helped mobilise for war.

Well, we're all part of Lippman's bewildered herd now. For those of us with aspirations to participate in democracy (or at least to feel as if we are participating), Crunch Time has compounded old problems and added new ones to those that Lippman identified a century ago, problems that go to the very heart of our democratic culture and threaten to make a farce of our claims to a civilised political culture. But the issue common to Lippman a century ago and us today is that we cannot disengage—democracy, for better or worse, is all we've got.

Why does democracy matter?

Democracy matters because government matters. Governments wield power and what they do (or don't do) impacts on all of us in the most fundamental ways. No matter how much energy any one of us puts into moulding the world, no matter how many street protests you attend or community initiatives you implement, a government edict can destroy those efforts with the stroke of a pen or the swing of a truncheon. To get to grips with the challenges that our societies will be facing in the twenty-first century we need to look at the system behind the pen stroke and the riot shield.

Arguing against democracy is a bit like taking Hitler's side in an argument: nice people don't do it. Democracy is the bottom line, if only because, as Churchill so famously observed, it is the worst system, except for all the rest. And it is a lousy system because democracies are destined to muddle through, to survive by trading interest against interest, horse against horse. Politicians in democracies are forced to take the middle ground, to water down their proposals and policies. There is no exhilarating vision for us all to march towards. But that isn't such a bad thing. Governments that are big on the 'vision thing' tend to build their success on the mass graves of those that disagree with them. During the twentieth century alone, government actions in countries that were strong on ideology— the Soviet Union, China and Cambodia, for instance—cost some 100 million lives, independent of the deaths caused in warfare, much of which was caused by ideological stridency. Self-inflicted massacres on these epic scales have been absent in democracies with their wishy-washy, middle-of-the-road politics and checks and balances on executive power.

Those wishy-washy, MOR politics and checks and balances may look bland and insipid from the outside, and can be ugly and damned frustrating on the inside, but they are remark-ably good at coming up with the kind of compromises and incremental progress that all the issues in this book need. The issue for us as fellow travellers through the twenty-first century will be how to maintain those checks and balances against the forces threatening to destroy them, from outside as well as in.

The 'domino theory' in reverse

How can democracy be in jeopardy? Hasn't it all been going democracy's way in the last part of the twentieth century? During the Cold War, the 'domino theory' held that once one country succumbed to communism the rest would follow. History's tide, and the power and inevitability of Karl Marx's vision, meant that an irresistible red wave would roll in and submerge the weak, bourgeois democracies.

It didn't quite work out like that.

In fact it pretty much happened in reverse. Over the last quarter of the twentieth century, one after the other—domino-style—authoritarian governments on the left and the right collapsed under the weight of their own internal inconsistencies. The process began in the mid-1970s in southern Europe's top holiday destinations, with the rightist military dictatorships in Portugal, Greece and Spain giving way to functioning democracies. In the 1980s democratic governments arrived in South America. Peru, Argentina, Uruguay, Brazil, Paraguay, Chile and, in 1990, Nicaragua all replaced bullets with ballots. In Asia, the Philippines dumped Marcos in 1986, and South Korea voted for voting the following year. There were democratic reforms in Taiwan, and huge, if ultimately unsuccessful, democratic protests in China and Burma. But the most dramatic switch was in Europe.

Communism's flagship totalitarian regime, the Soviet Union, had begun struggling internally from the 1970s. By the mid-1980s, the Soviet leader, Mikhail Gorbachev, tried to stop the rot with his policies of *perestroika* (restructuring) and *glasnost*

Democracy timeline

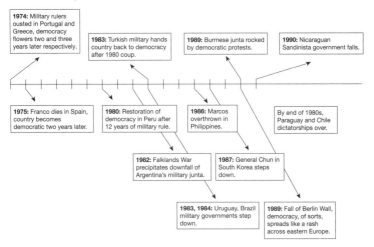

1974: Military rulers ousted in Portugal and Greece, democracy flowers two and three years later respectively.

1983: Turkish military hands country back to democracy after 1980 coup.

1989: Burmese junta rocked by democratic protests.

1990: Nicaraguan Sandinista government falls.

1975: Franco dies in Spain, country becomes democratic two years later.

1980: Restoration of democracy in Peru after 12 years of military rule.

1986: Marcos overthrown in Philippines.

By end of 1980s, Paraguay and Chile dictatorships over.

1982: Falklands War precipitates downfall of Argentina's military junta.

1987: General Chun in South Korea steps down.

1983, 1984: Uruguay, Brazil military governments step down.

1989: Fall of Berlin Wall, democracy, of sorts, spreads like a rash across eastern Europe.

(openness). His country responded by falling apart. The Soviet Union found itself unable to maintain its hold on its East European empire, its acolytes began breaking away, and with the symbolic fall of the Berlin Wall dividing communist East Germany from democratic West Germany in 1989, the communist dominoes began falling. Although in most cases the transition to any recognisable form of democracy has been complex and troubled—Yugoslavia, for instance, split into pieces and tore itself to bits—at the beginning of the twenty-first century the threadbare flag of liberal democracy flies from Warsaw to Vladivostok.

The collapse of communism caught academics by surprise. Some even had to revise their lecture notes. This huge number of historical transitions couldn't be just coincidence, but what was going on? Into this intellectual vacuum stepped Francis Fukuyama, an American professor who rolled up these events and saw an opportunity to turn Marxism on its head and make a name for himself. In the summer of 1989, as communism lay dying, he wrote an article proclaiming the 'End of History'.

The world is becoming more democratic

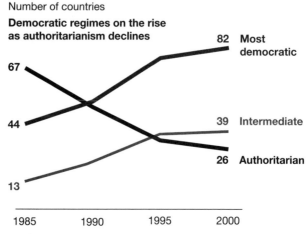

Number of countries
Democratic regimes on the rise
as authoritarianism declines

67

44

13

82 Most
democratic

39 Intermediate

26 Authoritarian

1985   1990   1995   2000

Source: Polity IV 2002.

Fukuyama argued that History (with a capital 'H') is the evolution of society to more advanced forms of civilisation—a
process that games-maker, Sid Meier, no doubt subscribes to.
More than that, History has come to an end because, with
communism calling it a day, liberal democracy is the only game
in town. Period.

History—it ends with a ballot, not a whimper

According to Fukuyama:

- As science makes breakthroughs, we simply know more
  about the world and evolve to a higher state of knowledge.
- Technology advances with science, and changes the way
  society is organised economically. As Marx said: 'The hand
  mill gives you society with the feudal lord; the steam mill,
  society with the industrial capitalist.' The only way to use

today's technology efficiently is through advanced industrialisation and a market-based economy. Societies that don't will be trampled by those that do.

- A market-based economy doesn't necessarily mean democracy. Think Singapore or China today, or Japan and Germany in the nineteenth century. *But*, a market-based economy does need better educated workers.
- Man is not just an economic animal—he needs other things apart from food, shelter and sex. He needs *recognition* of himself as a human being with value and worthy of respect, and this need for recognition grows with his level of education. The only political system that can ultimately provide this recognition to all citizens is liberal democracy.
- In the long run democracy wins. History ends. Next!

Well, maybe.

Market-based liberal democracy may yet turn out to be the end point of social evolution, but no one could deny that it has its problems, big ones. As a political system, democracy isn't even that peaceful and well-ordered in those countries that have had it the longest—it produces its fair share of inequities, injustice and conflict and, as we'll see later in the chapter, its legitimacy is constantly being threatened by real and significant structural problems. History with a small 'h' continues, and the crunch for us in democratic countries is how we organise ourselves to respond to the threats to our least-worst political systems from both the outside and the inside.

Democracy and its manipulators

You won't find it in any textbook, but the people who are the biggest threat to democracy drew their first principles from an event that occurred one night in October 1938. That evening, just after 8 p.m., a meteor slammed down in a field near Grover's Mill, New Jersey, causing a massive shockwave and blowing out a huge fiery crater. Radio reporter Carl Phillips was there and this was how he described it:

> Ladies and gentlemen,
>
> This is the most terrifying thing I have ever witnessed . . . Wait a minute! Someone's crawling. Someone or . . . something. I can see peering out of that black hole two luminous disks . . . Something's wriggling out of the shadow like a grey snake. Now it's another one, and another one, and another one. They look like tentacles to me. There, I can see the thing's body . . . The eyes are black and gleam like a serpent. The mouth is kind of V-shaped with saliva dripping from its rimless lips that seem to quiver and pulsate.

What Phillips had seen was part of an alien invasion force. The US Secretary of the Interior addressed the nation:

> I shall not try to conceal the gravity of the situation that confronts the country, nor the concern of your government in protecting the lives and property of its people . . . we must continue the performance of our duties, each and every one of us, so that we may confront this destructive adversary with a nation united, courageous, and consecrated to the preservation of human supremacy on this earth.

New York City was evacuated, roads were jammed, thousands leapt into the East River, cramming themselves onto boats and dinghies. The US Army was engaged, but very quickly overwhelmed. A final broadcast announced that the army had been obliterated—'artillery, air force, everything wiped out . . .'

Yes, this was a forerunner of the Roswell alien landing. The US administration hushed the whole thing up and . . .

Well, before you start wondering what drugs we're on, you've perhaps recognised this as a description of Orson Welles's radio adaptation of H.G. Wells's *The War of the Worlds*. Kidding aside, the program did actually fool tens of thousands of people into packing their things and running from the alien invasion, fearing the end of the world had arrived. What has all this to do with the state of our democracies? It's all about communication, darling.

The War of the Worlds was certainly good drama. Less well known, however, is that it was designed and carried out as an intricate experiment in government by social psychologist Paul Lazarsfeld. Lazarsfeld was interested in how people related to the stuff they heard on the radio. A German Jewish émigré who took Sigmund Freud's methods and wrapped them up in statistics, Lazarsfeld teamed up with Frank Stanton, another stats PhD and head of research at CBS, who was looking for new ways to figure out what made hit radio shows. Together, they developed the first rudimentary device for gauging radio listeners' preferences. For the first time in the history of modern communications, academics, media executives and sponsors joined together to understand what the public wanted and to give it to them.

It was this research that led to the broadcast of *The War of the Worlds*. Lazarsfeld looked into the characteristics of the broadcast and the nature of the panic that followed it. His conclusion may seem like a no-brainer when looked at through our sceptical twenty-first-century eyes, but at the time it was ground shaking. He found that the mass media was influential in shaping beliefs!

It may not sound like much, but at the time this stuff was gold to advertisers and broadcasters. Lazarsfeld's research and his findings have been carried through into the twenty-first century to become one of the most important influences in our democratic governance system. The *War of the Worlds* experiment led directly to those ubiquitous political tools: the focus group, the poll and spin. Which brings us to Edward Bernays.

Bernays had been a junior member of president Wilson's pro-war propaganda team, and he had more than a passing interest in psychology (Sigmund Freud was his uncle). Bernays took propaganda, his uncle's insights and Lippman's cynicism and created a new profession—public relations (see box).

Lazarsfeld's research and Welles's drama played straight into the world of PR created by Bernays, and since then it has been mainlined into our culture. Their insights into mass psychology have been used to sell everything from washing-up liquid to war. Bernays' career and those of his successors provide insight into wide and ongoing debates, many of which are often mistakenly conducted entirely in terms of the present but have been going on for decades. Take the current debate about corporate power (see chapter 8). Think it's new? Think again—the concerns of newspaper columnists of the 1920s

---

Selling bikinis to Eskimos

Edward Bernays' first publicity campaign was for Diaghilev's *Ballet Russe* on its 1915 US tour. It was a tricky assignment. Most Americans thought male ballet dancers were 'deviates'. Bernays undercut the prejudice, presenting magazine editors with articles asking: 'Are American men ashamed to be graceful?' From there Bernays moved on. During the First World War, as part of the War Department's Committee on Public Information, he conducted public information campaigns about the terms of the peace, and encouraged re-employment of returned servicemen. He built a huge PR business, with famous successes for Procter & Gamble (including the company's annual soap carving contest, designed to encourage children, the 'enemies of soap', to enjoy using it). Later, he infamously encouraged women to smoke in public, associating the practice with emancipation and freedom, a link which persists today, as indicated by the following quote taken from *The Guardian*:

> A friend was trying to give up cigarettes recently after more than 20 years of smoking. 'It's not the nicotine,' she said. 'It's the feeling I get of, "just fuck the lot of them."' A spare few minutes with a fag was the precious time she had for herself, free of the demands of children, work and boyfriend, she explained.

uncannily echo many of today's themes, such as overweening corporate power and the decline of the state. Or the current mass neurosis about political disaffection and apathy. Its roots lie in the counter-cultural movements of the left in the late 1960s, when people gave up on politics and turned inward to discover themselves.

Modern political strategists have learned from Bernays' extraordinary appropriation of psychoanalytical thinking to promote a concept of human nature that they can manipulate. Namely that we're nothing more than a bundle of irrational emotional responses and desires, often contradictory but ultimately—crucially—satiable. All that's required is the right buzz-word, the right image, the right product.

Today, accompanied by a phalanx of spin doctors, image consultants and public relations gurus, governments can fine-tune the messages they want us to absorb with frightening efficiency and ferocity. Want to feel manly? Use Lynx. Want to feel safe? Vote for the right. Want to feel solidarity? Vote for the left. Political preferences, like those for toothpaste, are now branded, branded, branded.

Manipulating democracy today

Guys like Lippman—originally working for Woodrow Wilson, one of America's most liberal, do-gooding presidents trying to make the world safe for democracy— Lazarsfeld and Bernays developed the black arts that threaten democracy today. In the Crunch Time world, those black arts combine frighteningly with the increasing dominance of the mass media. This nightmare was foreseen many decades ago, predicted by a writer who invented a world in which the media would dominate our daily lives, filling our minds with garbage that crowded out anything of significance. That writer was George Orwell and the book was *1984*. Orwell wrote in *1984* about the Ministry of Truth, the propaganda arm of the vicious totalitarian regime, and its role of manufacturing news for the 'proles':

> Here were produced rubbishy newspapers containing almost nothing except sport, crime and astrology . . .

Remind you of any newspapers you've read lately?

Orwell was right: media tycoons such as Rupert Murdoch and Silvio Berlusconi have made fortunes on *1984*'s ironic recipe of sport, crime and astrology for keeping the masses contented (Orwell thought they'd save sex for the movies— you can't be right about everything). Murdoch and Berlusconi have both used their empires to further political agendas—but only Italy's Berlusconi has used it to secure the leadership of his country. At the beginning of the twenty-first century, the average Italian soaks up more than four hours of TV a day. Providing their diet of sex, sport, crime and astrology is Prime Minister Berlusconi, with his three private Mediaset channels and the state broadcaster, RAI, indirectly controlled by the PM through his right-wing coalition's parliamentary majority. Italian journalists increasingly practise self-censorship, fearing they may lose their jobs if they are overcritical of Italy's richest man, their prime minister. Cases of 'improving' the news range from editing out prime ministerial 'gaffes' to airbrushing over his bald patch on the cover of *Panorama*, a weekly magazine.

How can a man with so much media power also be allowed to hold so much political power? He promised to change the law so that when he became prime minister his media interests would be quarantined in a way that would put them out of his reach. It is difficult enough to imagine how this might have happened had he been true to his word. Needless to say, he wasn't. But that isn't the worst of it. When he became prime minister in 2001, Berlusconi faced four criminal charges, in-cluding false accounting, illegal financing of a political party and bribing judges. One by one he managed to wriggle out of them through legal wrangling, refusal to cooperate or simply changing the law in his own favour. Remember, though, Italy is a democracy. People did actually have to go to the ballot and elect him. And they could vote him and his party out. You can't buy people in a democracy. Or can you?

Bernays, Lippman and Lazarsfeld put the lie to that innocent notion a long time ago. Money buys persuasion, and printing more election leaflets than the next guy pales in significance when it comes to owning your own TV networks, newspapers and publishing companies. Did we forget to mention Berlusconi owns Italy's biggest publisher with 30 per cent of the book market, that he controls 38 per cent of the magazine market, and owns the country's largest newspaper, *Il Giornale*? In his successful 2001 election campaign he sent out 12 million free copies of his autobiography.

Italy isn't the only democracy suffering from the effects of too much money in too few hands. In the US, during the 1999/2000 election cycle some $3 billion was spent to elect federal candidates. The politicians elected by these tidal waves of cash aren't just in hock to their donors. They're also pandered to by lobbyists with their own formidable financial resources. Politics and money have always been bedfellows, just as church and state used to be. It took several centuries for that link to be broken, the question is whether it will take two hundred years for campaign finance reform to sweep the democracies of the world. Let's face it, we don't have that long: it is, after all, Crunch Time.

So is there anything that might save us from being bought? Some people think there is. It begins with an E.

Education, education, education

Super-cynic Walter Lippman believed that society, with all its creases, folds and facets, is way too complex for voters to understand the real implications of their political choices. The

> Learning about democracy in school is like reading holiday
> brochures in prison.
>   Derry Hannam, British educationalist

great Victorian thinker John Stuart Mill thought the necessary
pre-condition of universal suffrage was compulsory secondary
education.

What do we need today? Should a working knowledge of
statistics be required? Or an exam for potential voters, like a
driving test? Should your vote, as a person intelligent and
curious enough to get at least halfway through a complex book
such as this one (or be lucky enough to open it at such an interesting page), be worth more than someone whose last claim to
reading was the label on a beer can? When it comes to education the democratic waters get pretty muddy.

Political philosophers have been hung up about education
since ancient Greece. The idea of education in a democracy is
to make us all think differently. Education, argue the theorists,
produces informed disagreement, however bitter. Without it
we are simply flying without instruments.

American thinker John Dewey wrote *Democracy and
Education* at around the time Walter Lippman was rallying
Americans to join the Western Front. Dewey thought education
was the glue that held democracy together, a shared experience
that would help us all appreciate one another's points of
view. Perhaps he was overstating the case, but as we saw in
the 'Science' chapter, and as we shall see when we look at
'Security', there is no doubt that the more we understand about
the world, the more crucial our democratic institutions become.
Dewy said:

> The devotion of democracy to education is a familiar fact. The
> superficial explanation is that a government resting upon popular
> suffrage cannot be successful unless those who elect and who

> obey their governors are educated . . . But there is a deeper
> explanation. A democracy is more than a form of government; it
> is primarily a mode of associated living, of conjoint communi-
> cated experience.

Even so, Lippman knew that education may give us more understanding, but it doesn't prevent us from following our irrational, animal instincts (even world-famous Cambridge physicist Stephen Hawking gets photographed in lap-dancing joints). We are lured easily into endorsing decisions by slogans, ads, posters, sound bites, TV spots—we buy wars as willingly as we buy trainers. Is democracy just a fancy name for the system that vested interests use to manipulate us?

Globalisation . . . again

The quality of our governance has always been threatened by the ability of those with money, means and know-how to employ sophisticated (and not so sophisticated) techniques to influence our opinions. But these concerns are now joined by a new and seemingly ubiquitous one: globalisation. As Thomas Friedman says in *The Lexus and the Olive Tree*:

> Your economy grows and your politics shrinks . . . the Golden
> Straightjacket narrows the political and economic policy choices
> of those in power to relatively tight parameters. That is why it is
> increasingly difficult these days to find any real differences
> between ruling and opposition parties in those countries that
> have put on the Golden Straightjacket. Once your country puts
> it on, its political choices get reduced to Pepsi or Coke—to slight
> nuances of taste. Slight nuances of policy, slight alterations in
> design to account for local traditions, some loosening here or
> there, but never any major deviation from the core golden rules.

In the 'Environment' chapter we saw how America's love of the SUV threatens floods, hurricanes and drought as far away as Mozambique or Switzerland. In the 'Security' chapter we will see how violent local disputes can get played out on the world stage. In 'People, People, People' we'll see how another country's fertility rate can very soon create trouble in our own backyard. Crunch Time issues are simply beyond the reach of many of our democratically elected governments. With globalisation our own actions reach across borders in a way that makes democratic governance irrelevant. We buy timber or diamonds or oil which prop up corrupt regimes abroad, or bankroll lobbyists for big corporations at home. As the crowds of protestors outside the G12 meetings will only too willingly agree, globalisation poses a huge threat to democratic accountability. Why? Because we vote within the structures of a nation state, while global issues batter away at our ability to control what goes on without so much as a democratic nod or whistle.

A financial scandal in Houston hits Arthur Andersen employees in major cities around the world. Our democratically elected representatives can tantrum about it all they like, but nurses, teachers, assembly plants and call centres are shipped from continent to continent, leaving us, back home, without health, education or jobs. The bits of our lives controlled by our democratic institutions, be they parliament or congress, senate or bundestag, are getting smaller as we write and you read. In the 'Globalisation' chapter, we will see how countries which do not adopt the neo-liberal agenda in their economies are cut out of the wash of global funds. What politician can afford to promote a policy that will cut his country off from the global financial system and the billions of dollars of foreign investment it offers? None that expects to remain in office. In globalisation circles, this has become known as the 'Golden Straitjacket'. If you wear it the right way (the neo-liberal way), it apparently comes with great financial rewards. But once you've got it on, freedom of movement is, well . . . restricted. Whether it makes countries richer or simply more volatile, the

Golden Straitjacket and the policies it implies undeniably cut down the range of policies our governments are able to propose or implement.

If you are feeling disempowered by the political process, it is because politicians long ago admitted defeat in the face of the seemingly overwhelming power of globalisation. In Australia, it began with Bob Hawke, as the one-time trade unionist held the white flag to the global financial markets and implemented a string of liberalising and deregulating reforms which continued through the Keating and Howard years, from floating the dollar and striking a wages accord to deregulating the banks and implementing a goods and services tax. The country might be financially better off as a result (and it might not) but who can argue that left-winger Hawke and his successor would have followed these policies if right-wing Thatcher and Reagan had not.

The world beyond our borders has often forced its way into our lives. War, trade, diplomacy—these things have always materially changed people's circumstances. Think of the bizarre fate of thousands of Australians dying in a European war on the shores of Turkey. Back then it was hard to understand the connection between Sydney and Gallipoli. Today the two countries do about half a billion dollars worth of trade every year. But it's not just commercial connections that count. It's the things that people do within their own borders that affect us materially.

The influences that touch our lives are global, but our politics remain (in)effectively local. The old feudal aristocracy was tied to land. Dukes and counts were always of somewhere—a piece of land, a place on the map. Feudalism may have disappeared but democracy, by necessity—almost by definition—keeps its love of the land alive. Our representatives remain resolutely tied to geography, which limits their ability to respond to the global influences that increasingly shape our lives.

But this presents us with an immense paradox. We need strong international institutions to solve the big global problems Crunch Time is presenting us with: global warming, the seepage of nuclear weaponry, an international water crisis and the rest. But the creation of such institutions implies a loss of the democratic accountability that is so crucial to maintaining healthy societies. Even now, at the beginning of the twenty-first century, much of the power our democracies gave to national parliaments lies in some foreign city with some institution we only know as some obscure acronym: EU, UN, APEC, WTO . . . the list goes on. The power hasn't evaporated, but the democratic accountability has.

According to democracy advocates, whenever our leaders sign up for a big international agreement they give up a little of the power that we gave up to them. Today that means agreements. Not just on old-fashioned things like military alliances, it means environment protocols, farm subsidies, accounting standards—you name it, they've signed up to it. The voters have been squeezed out again.

What does this mean for us? It means that broad, global Crunch Time issues will be the source of increasing friction throughout the next century.

Democracy's Disneyland

High above the hills of Lake Zurich sits Kilchberg, a busy, innocent little place, home to about 7000 people. It's the headquarters of Lindt chocolate, but chocolate has little to do with the future of democracy. What does is what goes on in Kilchberg itself, a model that perhaps all democracies could work towards—a method of local government that encourages and rewards citizenship and community involvement and is clearly transparent and democratically accountable.

The community holds all the powers that haven't been specifically given over to the regional or federal government.

A quarter of all the taxes people pay go to Kilchberg itself, via income and property levies. The town educates its kids up to the age of 16, and does everything from build the school to elect the committee that hires the teachers. It hands out cash to its poor and to a handful of refugees. It has a volunteer fire brigade. The local police run a couple of patrol cars in town and a couple of boats on the lake. There's a retirement home and a community farm with an honesty box. And it's all run by seven elected councillors—that's one to every thousand voters—who supervise a small team of professionals.

But that's not why Kilchberg is so great. The real kicker is that four times a year the seven people who run it have to present their recommendations to a town meeting and let the voters decide on what to do. These meetings fix taxes, pass new laws, check the accounts and okay planning proposals. Anything else anybody wants to bring up can be discussed. This is direct democracy. Want to vote? Raise your hand. Want a paper ballot, fine, but a third of people must agree. If you don't like the council's ideas, go and get 15 signatures and put a new proposal to your fellow voters. A single person can demand a specific action from the council with the right, if the council does not agree, to take the matter up to the cantonal and federal levels. The only time that's happened was when someone wanted the community farm to go organic.

Before you roll your eyes at this cheesier-than-Swiss-cheese story, it would be well worth noting that the world's only superpower is also built of little communities just like this one. In America, town meetings are used to elect almost all municipal officials, from the town clerk and sexton through to the school district treasurer and the head of the Parents and Teachers Association. A century and a half ago Alexis de Tocqueville, travelling French aristo, noted in *Democracy in America* that:

> Town meetings are to liberty what primary schools are to science; they bring it within people's reach, they teach men how to use

and enjoy it. A nation may establish a free government, but
without municipal institutions it cannot have the spirit of liberty.

It is that spirit of liberty that is missing when we feel disempowered and disillusioned by the weakness of our vote. When our communities and families are affected by swirling global forces, the problem is compounded by the giving away of control of those parts of our own lives which should rightfully be ours, and we become disengaged from the only communities we have direct control over—our own. The way forward is to take back those controls, to actively inject life back into our local communities, to access the energy that has been stolen from us by the everyday demands of being a person in the twenty-first century and to reinject that through democracy into others.

Democracy means that power is vested in the people, and given upwards only where necessary. It means that the person who decides how heavy the juggernauts are that trundle through my neighbourhood should not be based in Canberra but in my town, aware of the weight the neighbourhood's roads can hold, and hopefully elected and approved by me. This does two things; it makes me feel in control of my life, and it gives the road person an important and empowering job. The bureaucrat in Canberra will still have plenty of lunch to do.

What is interesting is how the principles of local democracy mirror those we discussed in the 'Environment' chapter, when we were looking at the concept of environmental sustainability. There are three principles that indicate an enterprise has a shot at being sustainable—they are generally local in nature, they purposefully enforce low inequality, and they are in it for the long run. The same could be said of local democracy. Coming together as a community and discussing the issues that matter in our lives gives people ownership over them. If we cannot do anything major about global warming, we can at least fix the broken window at the bus stop, or organise a fundraiser for the local hostel.

Democracy's flexibility

Of course we live different lives now than we did when de Tocqueville was visiting America. Frankly there is hardly enough time to do the things you need to do, let alone attend a rambling and time-consuming meeting about the status of the municipal toilets. Even in Kilchberg, no more than about 400 people generally turn up at town meetings, maybe 700 when something especially exciting is on the menu. As a percentage of the community's 4000 qualified voters, that is small. The answer lies in two things: the use of new technology, particularly the all-pervasive Internet, and new forms of democratic governance to help us address some of the broader issues.

Instead of politicians pushing our buttons perhaps we should be pushing theirs. For the past two hundred years—except in the odd Swiss canton—democracy has meant a system by which people vote every few years to elect a handful of representatives, who in between elections make all the important decisions—war, peace, taxes, the lot (hence Adrian's point about global anti-war protests . . . a waste of time). Technology now offers us the opportunity for something more direct, more fully 'democratic'—decisions by the vote of the whole people through the Internet, perhaps. Which ought to set Walter Lippman rolling in his grave.

Lippman once noted the practical justification for representative democracy was that people needed their betters to represent them. Now representatives say it's because of separation of roles—we, the people, are actually too busy to govern the country (although a look at empty seats in assembly chambers will show that often our representatives are too). But during the last half of the twentieth century, most people in the Western democracies have gotten themselves better educated, more money, and more free time to think about what goes on around them. They're better informed too, and are used to discussing issues as broad and varied as the impact of genetically modified foods on the environment, the justification for the invasion of Iraq, or the plots and sub-plots of *The Sopranos* episode by episode.

In time, people will grow to expect more from their democratic system than that which is being delivered, and challenge the structures of representative democracy. The Internet with appropriate checks and balances in place will eventually provide reliable methods for validating electronic votes, and it will remove the biggest single obstacle to direct democracy—the physical difficulty of distributing information to a large population, engaging it in debate and collecting its votes. In light of these developments, many people will come to see national elections every few years as a totally blunt instrument for expressing the popular will, a remnant from the age of steam when most representative institutions were invented.

Just ask

Pollsters regularly ask our opinion on issues of state, and elected representatives pay attention to what the opinion polls say. Everywhere, ordinary people are now in a better position to examine what their representatives are up to, observe their voting records, web pages or personal problems. They can conclude for themselves whether it's really a good idea to let this pathetic shower choose so many of our policies. The politicians seem to be making the same choices too. People are no longer willing to offer the deference representatives once expected.

What's more, Swiss-style direct democracy may be better than the representative sort at coping with one of the chief weaknesses of modern politics—lobbying. In the relatively humdrum, de-ideologised politics of post-communist days, the lobbyist is getting even more powerful than he used to be; and democrats are right to be worried.

Lobbying has an important role to play in policy-making. People who make decisions in any field should be party to as much argument and debate as possible. But Lippman and Bernays taught us how persuasive persuasion can be. Lobbying goes wrong when special interests use their money to cross the line between persuading politicians and pocketing them. In dealing with a relatively small handful of elected politicians, the lobbyist has many ways of doing that, ranging from 'entertainment' through to the manila envelope stuffed with cash or the legal donation of millions into campaign funds. But when lobbyists face an entire electorate, bribery and vote buying are more difficult. Advertising billboards and 30-second slots replace cosy chats in clubby corners.

Wealthy media tycoons can help voters make dumb decisions. For the big issues this will always be so. But the lesson here is that we need to take control where we can, to drag the power back down to a level where we can exert influence over the forces that impact our lives. Yes, we will make mistakes, but at least they will be our mistakes, not those of some infuriatingly unseen bureaucrat or smug politician. The more political responsibility ordinary people are given, the more responsibly most of them will vote, goes the mantra. Direct democracy, with a little technology, may help to produce something closer to true government by the people. And that, after all, is the way the logic of Crunch Time points. Democracy's cheerleaders and ideologists spent much of the last century telling totalitarians and dictators that they ought to trust the people. Now it's time for them to trust us.

North Shore Against the War

Bay Street, Mosman, is an unlikely bed of revolutionary unrest. Leafy and affluent, overlooking a gorgeous inlet of inner Sydney

Harbour with the marvellously twee moniker Quaker's Hat Bay, it would ordinarily be only notable for a much higher than average quota of SUV-driving mums and merchant-banking residents. Sue and David Roffey, however, have made it the epi-centre of exactly the kind of grass-roots democratic movement that De Tocqueville was so enthusiastic about, and which supports communities such as Kilchberg. It began when Sue found herself 'incandescent with rage' over the Howard government's approach to the impending invasion of Iraq in 2003.

'I put a little ad in the local paper saying, "I'm opposed to war, is anyone else?" with our telephone number, and the next week we had a half a dozen people around our dinner table discussing what to do,' she says.

The first objective was to raise awareness for the anti-war march coming up on 16 February. The Roffeys had taken part in an earlier march in November 2002 that had attracted 10 000 people, but had been disappointed because a lot of people who would have attended the march had not found out about it early enough to go. The dinner table group decided to print a leaflet and take them to the Mosman market the following weekend, together with some information placards and some purple ribbons—a symbol of peace—for supporters to buy and wear.

Expecting to attract abuse in the staunchly blue-ribbon elec-torate, the Roffeys were thrilled and overwhelmed with the level of support that day. Donations came thick and fast, $600 in all. They used the money to print T-shirts for the march—'North Shore Against the War' on the front and 'Think again John' on the back—helping to create both a sense of community and a really visible presence. Other small victories followed.

The group managed to get a unanimous vote in Mosman Council—one of the country's most conservative—against the war—'Astonishing', as Sue put it. A student offered to set up the group's website www.sydneypeace.com, including a noticeboard for peace groups across the city, which also had minutes of the group's meetings, notices of upcoming events, facts about the war and links to other relevant sites. They built an emailing list of some 300 names. One of the group's members was very active campaigning against the use of cluster bombs, contributing to a senate pronouncement against Australia using the weapons.

Still, the group and their 250 000 fellow marchers in Sydney failed to prevent the war. But as the tanks were nearing Baghdad in April, David Roffey and another member of North Shore Against the War went to see their local MP, Tony Abbott. Against expectations, it was an interesting two-way dialogue.

'I think he was expecting to nod his head a lot and bid us goodbye, but in the end we had a long conversation. He admitted that he had told parliament that invading Iraq might increase terrorism, and that Cabinet had come down on him for it. More than that, he said he didn't feel there was enough debate in Australian politics,' reported David.

So they asked whether he would be willing to front a public discussion of the issues in six months, once the war was over. Abbott said yes. The forum organised for later in the year helped attract the attention of a well-known Sydney journalist, Margo Kingston, who helped the group publicise the event and publish an article in a Sunday paper. In October, Abbott faced down a packed North Sydney Council Hall, and the Roffeys were turning people away at the door. Inside, a panel of four, including Abbott, Labor MP Tanya Plibersek, former independent candidate Peter MacDonald and Donna Mulhearn, a human shield in Iraq, were asked six questions distilled from the hundreds received from the peace group's mailing list. The session got coverage in the media (not nearly enough, thought the Roffeys) and a transcript was put up on the group's website.

Now renamed North Shore Peace and Democracy, the group meets monthly and is tackling issues such as the Australia–US Free Trade Agreement, negotiated behind closed doors and presented to the public as a fait accompli, and the role of the media in protecting our democratic rights. Sue and David have some tips for aspiring democrats:

1   **Manage meetings:** Democratic meetings can be stiflingly long-winded and rambling if not chaired properly, and they need to follow some rules if they are going to achieve anything. They need to model the kind of democracy you want to build, one in which everybody is heard and all ideas are considered. Contributions should be actively positive: 'Yes, and . . .', not 'Yes, but'. Less, 'I think you ought to . . .' and more 'I will . . .'. People need to feel as if they are being listened to, otherwise they won't come back. This is what community action is about, respect and democracy.

2   **The work must be shared:** There is an enormous amount to do organising any sort of collective action, let alone a public discussion with politicians, the media and the rest. If any one person's life is impacted in a detrimental way they will simply stop participating, and before long the whole thing will have petered out. To keep the momentum going, the work has to be shared out between people so everyone has something to do and nobody too much. North Shore Peace and Democracy has a strong core of about 10 to 12 regular participants, each of whom shoulders their part of the organisational hassle. That way it becomes manageable and we and everyone else in the group still manage to have a life outside.

3   **If you are angry, _do_ something about it:** Silent acquiescence is collusion or, as Martin Luther King put it, 'Our lives begin to end the day we become silent about things that matter.' 'I was beside myself with anger about what was happening,' says Sue, 'and used the energy that anger gave me. If I hadn't done something I'd have felt even worse.'

The group and its activities make the couple feel more comfortable about their neighbourhood. While it might be SUV-mum/merchant-banker territory, the area is composed of a diverse group of people who do feel passionately about issues. Only usually they don't give themselves permission to speak up about them.

5
SECURITY

There is no single driving force behind the urge toward civilization, no one goal toward which every culture strives. There is, instead, a web of forces and objectives that impel and beckon, shaping cultures as they grow . . . five basic impulses are of the greatest importance to the health and flexibility of your fledgling society: exploration, economics, knowledge, conquest, and culture.

A winning strategy is one that combines all of these aspects into a flexible whole. Your first mission is to survive; your second is to thrive. It is not true that the largest civilization is necessarily the winner, nor that the wealthiest always has the upper hand. In fact, a balance of knowledge, cash, military might, cultural achievement, and diplomatic ties allows you to respond to any crisis that occurs, whether it is a barbarian invasion, an aggressive rival, or an upsurge of internal unrest.

Civilization III User's Guide: 'Introduction'

In Sid Meier's computer game, *Civilization*, combatants can stamp their mark on the world in a number of ways. They can conquer their enemies through military strength, economic domination, technological and scientific advances, or through cultural domination. Statecraft and diplomacy—which countries to cosy up to, and which to wage war against—are key skills.

The security story that dominates our attention at the beginning of the twenty-first century is the result of the current state of play in our own macro-civilisation and there is no doubt that one particular player is way out in front. As this century began, one twentieth of the world's people produced nearly a third of the world's economic output. Militarily, that twentieth spent close to US$1 billion a day arming itself against the remaining 95 per cent of us (that's roughly a third of total world military expenditure). Intellectually, it shelled out 15 per cent of the global research budget. Culturally it raked in over 50 per cent of what the world spent on watching movies. That twentieth of the world's people comprises a coherent, organised body: the United States of America. Take a look at the chart on page 122.

In almost every sphere, what America thinks and does dominates. It isn't too much to say that the Crunch Time security story will be America's attempts to maintain its position against the other nineteen-twentieths of the world.

Maintain the disparity

The twenty-first may not be America's century. The high water mark of American power has already passed:

> We have 50 per cent of the world's wealth, but only 6.3 per cent of its population. In this situation, our real job in the coming period is to devise a pattern of relationships that permit us to maintain this disparity. To do so, we have to dispense with all sentimentality . . . we should cease thinking about human rights, the raising of living standards and democratization.

Only the numbers let slip that this isn't the latest memo from the White House's national security adviser. In fact it was

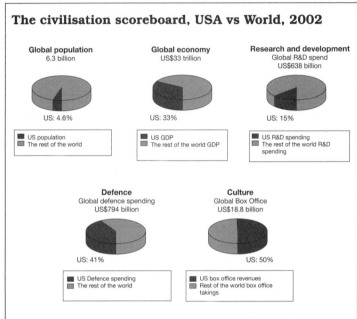

The civilisation scoreboard, USA vs World, 2002

Global population
6.3 billion

US: 4.6%

■ US population
▨ The rest of the world

Global economy
US$33 trillion

US: 33%

■ US GDP
▨ The rest of the world GDP

Research and development
Global R&D spend
US$638 billion

US: 15%

■ US R&D spending
▨ The rest of the world R&D spending

Defence
Global defence spending
US$794 billion

US: 41%

■ US Defence spending
▨ The rest of the world

Culture
Global Box Office
US$18.8 billion

US: 50%

■ US box office revenues
▨ Rest of the world box office takings

Sources: Population Reference Bureau; EIU; Stockholm International Peace Institute; European Union Institute for Security Studies; OECD; Democratic Caucus on Science; Motion Picture Association of America; Australian Film Commission. Thanks to Sue Watts of Bestofbiz.com.

written in the late 1940s by one of America's top diplomats, George Kennan. As we saw above, America today may have comparatively less wealth and less people, but the fundamental reality underlying American policy remains the same: maintain the disparity.

This chapter is our attempt to make sense of the increasingly complex security issues that are appearing in the newspapers at the beginning of the twenty-first century, and the sensible response to the global picture for the individual. But the story doesn't start in the Pentagon. It starts in South-East Asia.

Trouble in paradise

American couple Martin and Gracia Burnham weren't used to luxury. As operatives for the zealous New Tribes Mission, their singular purpose in life was to bring the gospel of Jesus Christ to remote people in remote places, a call Martin had been answering since childhood with his parents in the Philippines. That meant a life spent camping out in the jungle and dining on the occasional malnourished chicken.

So when it came to celebrating their eighteenth wedding anniversary they took a break from roughing it and headed for Arreceffi Island and the five-star beach bungalows and gourmet buffets of the Dos Palmas resort. Sited in the tropical waters of the southern Philippines, it's a serene world unto itself. Tastefully appointed huts rest on stilts above a clear blue bay. There are picnic lunches on the water, infinity pools and jet spas, and snorkelling in pristine coral reefs. Dos Palmas offers the complete international luxury tourist experience, removed from the everyday cares of real life. There was one aspect of real life, however, the international luxury tourist experience couldn't block out.

On Sunday morning, 27 May 2001, the Burnhams were roughly woken as armed bandits slammed a boat onto the resort's beach. The gunmen headed for the tastefully appointed huts, grabbed the Burnhams, some other guests off the beach and a number of resort staff. Coralling twenty people into the boat, they headed north towards the scores of jungle islets that dot that part of the world.

Pursued by planes, helicopters and patrol boats, the bandits were eventually tracked to the jungle island of Basilan, where at one stage they were cornered in a hospital. They escaped, but added a local nurse to their hostage collection. Over the course of the next few months hostages were released and killed until the diminishing group consisted only of the kidnappers, the nurse and the Burnhams. In Basilan, it really is a jungle out there.

The Burnhams' capture and pursuit was to become a pivotal event in the unfolding 'war against terror', but not because the Burnhams were in any way significant. American hostages had dominated the US political scene since the seizure of the US embassy in Tehran and the kidnappings of US citizens in Lebanon. The Philippines, however, is not part of the volatile landscape of the Middle East. Attention rapidly focused on what the most powerful state in the world would do for its captive citizens.

For a long time, not a lot. In November 2001, six months after their capture, a local Filipino TV station broadcast a video clip of the Burnhams, looking exhausted and desperate. In the intervening period, nothing had changed for them. But while they were being shunted from jungle hideout to jungle hideout, everything had changed for America.

People as pawns

Around the time of the Burnhams' interview, two things were happening that would have a grave bearing on their fate. First, following September 11 and America's attack on Afghanistan, the Bush administration was trying to define the notion of a 'war on terrorism'. They knew they had to fight terrorists other than bin Laden's al-Qaeda, but the question was, 'Which ones?' Second, the Philippines' president, Gloria Macapagal-Arroyo, was visiting Washington. She had come with a deal. The US could use her air and naval bases. In exchange she wanted 'help' with a domestic terrorist problem, and about US$100 million worth of military hardware.

Arroyo presented the bandit gang who'd snatched the Burnhams as a domestic terrorism problem. But in actual fact the kidnappers were disaffected youths who happened to be Muslims with an Arabic name (Abu Sayyaf, meaning 'sword-bearer'). They were led by a charismatic 40-year old who went by the *nomme de guerre* of Abu Sabaya, and wore Oakley wrap-around shades. Originally a criminology student, he'd left the Philippines to work in Saudi Arabia and had been drawn into Islamist circles that took him to Libya and Pakistan. This was enough for the Americans: the Muslim connection was clear. The Burnhams' kidnappers were no longer just local thugs, they were the new front in the 'war on terror', and US cash and support was quickly forthcoming.

The Philippines constitution forbids foreign forces from operating on its soil, but three months after the Burnhams' weary TV appearance, over a thousand US 'military advisers' arrived in Basilan to 'train' their Philippine colleagues in jungle warfare. Four months after they'd arrived the 'training' paid off, as did US-supplied helicopter gunships and night-vision equipment. The US-backed forces cornered the gang and their three hostages in a remote ravine. The Burnhams' drama seemed like it was about to end.

What to make of all this?

The question for us, just getting on with our lives, is what to make of terrible events such as these—how to make sense of them in a way that adds meaning rather than confusion. The Burnhams' story made good newspaper copy. It had drama and tension, and could be slotted easily into wider events in the world (the 'war on terror'). But the issue for us now is less about the news qualities of the Burnhams than the insight their tragic tale provides us into the forces that shape our world—how those forces work together to change our lives, and how we in turn can work to influence them. How, in fact, we should behave in a world where you can be snatched from an idyllic holiday retreat and sucked into a local power struggle that, in turn, is just a part of a global diplomatic game.

That is where our argument began.

'This is a classic case of American imperialism,' Adrian was saying over the phone one night. 'The Burnhams were an irrelevant, but fortunate, detail for the politicians. The Filipinos would have got their money and the Americans their bases, Burnhams or no Burnhams,' he continued. 'Remember, Bush had just bombed the daylights out of Afghanistan. He was looking for a second front, somewhere to demonstrate that the "war against terror" is a global fight. The Philippines was the ideal solution—a friendly country in need of some help to quell some local trouble from independence-minded rebels of an Islamic persuasion. More than that, South-East Asia is somewhere strategic analysts have been twitchy over for decades. A "rescue mission" was the perfect excuse to send in troops and secure a crucial part of the American empire.'

Mike disagreed. 'You don't have to like Bush and his lot to realise that a country, especially a superpower, has a duty to protect its citizens. Terrorism, even of the kind demonstrated by the Burnhams' kidnappers, poses an enormous threat, not just to the US, but to all societies that value freedom of thought and liberal ideals,' he went on. 'September 11 was the worst and most shocking example, but as an activity in general, terrorism works against everything our societies stand for, it threatens lives and infrastructure, and also the way we relate to each other, our tolerance and understanding. America is one of the few countries with the power to combat it. Let's be thankful for that. There is a big political game going on but policy is also about trying to protect people like the Burnhams, trying to react to September 11, the Bali bombings and everything else that happens.

'More than that,' he added, 'look at the facts specific to South-East Asia. Two of the September 11 hijackers had spent time in Malaysia. Ramzi Yousef, the mastermind of the first bombing of the World Trade Center in 1993, used the Philippines as a base, and it was thought that al-Qaeda may regroup in South-East Asia. In these circumstances, President Arroyo's invitation was a golden opportunity for the US to track down and destroy terrorists affiliated to the broad anti-American alliance, it stopped that alliance from gaining a foothold in a new, important and volatile part of the world and extended a helping hand to a friend in need, and supported a fledgling democratic regime that had replaced the Marcos dictatorship.'

The conversation continued over the next few days. Adrian accused Mike of being naïve, thinking that there was no grand plan. 'It is ridiculous to believe that President Bush and his advisers react to daily events without having some broader idea of where history is going. As if punch and counter-punch was all that matters. As if the phalanx of analysts in the Pentagon and the spin doctors who replay every move the President makes for the public have no grander plan than re-election.'

He sent Mike a quote from Lord Curzon, who ruled India at the end of the nineteenth century:

> I confess that countries are pieces on a chessboard upon which is being played out a great game for the domination of the world.

He pointed to a list of American 'interventions' between 1945 and 2000: 201 different theatres in 55 years, according to the Federation of American Scientists. 'Taken together,' reckoned Adrian, 'they look like a sustained military campaign, the exercise of imperial muscle.'

Mike had to agree, taken together it does look like there is an empire thing going on here. But they can't be taken together. 'Anti-communism prompted the Berlin airlift. Bill Clinton's liberal interventionism took US forces into Kosovo. Both these "imperialist" actions were just responses to other people's moves. Stalin blockaded Berlin. Milosevic invaded Kosovo. The US just decided not to sit back. It did something. For which both Berliners and Kosovans were pretty damn grateful. Lord Curzon was living in a different age,' reckoned Mike. 'It's Crunch Time, and our times are better described by a British prime minister from the 1950s, Harold Macmillan. When asked by a reporter what he most feared, Macmillan answered,

"Events, dear boy, events",' said Mike. 'Events, not conspiracies, drive the big security issues of our time.'

Agreeing to disagree, we labelled our respective positions.

Adrian's global chessboard

The world is run by a powerful and elite group of politicians, corporate bosses, government officials and bureaucrats, assisted by the World Bank, the International Monetary Fund (IMF) and other odious institutions. These individuals and institutions have a single-minded objective: to maintain the disparity. They want to hang on to power and increase their own influence and wealth. They use any means possible: military 'intervention', ownership of the media, restriction of personal rights, repressive legal systems, the lot, and internationally they enforce systems that increase inequality and injustice such as third-world indebtedness, taxation systems that benefit the wealthy and straightforward crony capitalism.

Conspiracy?

Mike's events

The world is the way it is through a combination of historical accident and human nature. People are generally well intentioned, although sometimes they make bad decisions or focus on the wrong things. Elected politicians want their policies and reforms to benefit society as a whole, but face choices that sometimes conflict with other closely held beliefs. Our political leaders are also the guardians of our national security. One of their gravest responsibilities is to keep us safe, both now and into the future.

Business chiefs believe they are adding value to the world we live in, economically and socially. They provide jobs for employees and profits for shareholders who in turn invest in other valuable enterprises. Institutions such as the World Bank and the IMF mean well and their mistakes are usually visible only with hindsight. Their poor image is the result of a lazy and cynical public happy to give a credit card number but not a helping hand.

Naïve?

The question we need to answer is which of these two worlds we actually live in. Which of these scenarios is more useful when it comes to making sense of global security issues on the one hand and personal crises like the Burnhams' on the other?

The strategic background

Earlier in this chapter we met George Kennan, who wrote that the US main strategic focus had to be on maintaining the disparity between America and the rest of the world. That quote comes from a document known as the 'Long Telegram'. It was sent from the US embassy in Moscow in February 1946, where Kennan was posted, to the State Department. It began drily: 'In view of recent events, the following remarks will be of interest to the department'. The telegram proceeded to outline, in over 6000 words, the looming threat to the western world from the dogmatic and confrontational ideology of Soviet Russia. Kennan's strategic insights set the stage for the ensuing half-century. As Stalin said in 1927, addressing a delegation of American workers:

> There will emerge two centres of world significance: a socialist centre, drawing to itself the countries which tend towards socialism, and a capitalist centre, drawing to itself the countries that incline towards capitalism. Battle between these two centres for command of world economy will decide fate of capitalism and of communism in entire world.

After the Second World War, the back end of the twentieth century was held together by the precarious balance of power between the United States and the Soviet Union. Staring each other down across the Iron Curtain, their mutual antagonism provided each with a focal point for their interaction with the rest of the world. The Americans sought to contain the Soviets, and the Soviets fought to maintain their grip on the regions of the world under communist influence.

There were events—the Cuban missile crisis, Vietnam, Afghanistan—but these were also chess moves, tactics determined by broad strategic imperatives (think *Civilization*—cash, weaponry, technology, culture and diplomacy) with moves explained in terms referring to the fundamental ideological differences between the capitalism of the west and the communism of the Soviet Union. If Senator McCarthy was hunting down communists at home, it was only logical that the President of the US should be hunting them (or at least 'containing' them) abroad.

Nuclear Armageddon was avoided perhaps because of mutually assured destruction—the two powers had a combined arsenal powerful enough to destroy the entire globe fifty times over. Or perhaps not. Maybe we were just lucky. In any case, the indisputable fact after the fall of the Berlin Wall in November 1989 was that America won the Cold War. For many commentators, it won not because of the brilliance of its strategic planners, and not because of the superiority of its military prowess, but because of the inherent ability of its capitalist economic system to produce growth (see chapter 1, 'Money and work'), and the sheer political strain of the Soviet Union maintaining a totalitarian state (see chapter 4, 'Democracy'). The Soviet Union simply could not afford to spend as much money on arms as the US—it had enough trouble getting its bakers to bake bread.

Cause for celebration for the west as that may have been, the side effect of the collapse of the Soviet Union was the collapse of the stabilising, if repressive, influence of the Cold War. From Russia in the west through to China in the east, states in central Asia that had fallen squarely under the influence of the communists were now free to bargain with whomever they liked. And they had a lot to bargain with.

It is against this background that the events of the early part of the twenty-first century have played themselves out, and it is against this that we must analyse which of our theories is closer to the truth.

A game of chess

History is the sum of big deeds and small. Sometimes it takes distance to determine what was truly historic—a decisive capture on the chessboard—and what was just noise.

When Austria's Archduke Franz Ferdinand and his wife were shot dead by the Miljacka River in the centre of Sarajevo it began the chain of events that led to the First World War. That was historic. Eighty years later that same river flanked the no-man's land off Sarajevo's 'sniper's alley'. Many more than just two people were shot dead, but no global war ensued. That was noise—tragic and heart-breaking, but just noise.

The difficulty as we open our newspapers each day is to determine what is historic, and what is just noise.

When Archduke Ferdinand was assassinated on that bridge in Sarajevo it was, from this distance, a defining moment in the twentieth century. But even from this close, whichever way you cut it, September 11, 2001 was an equally momentous day: a day that altered our entire strategic background. When hijacked aircraft destroyed Manhattan's tallest buildings and took a chunk out of the Pentagon they destroyed the myth of the American heartland's invulnerability. For America as a nation, it marked a new and frightening stage in its grand game of civilisation—it demonstrated its weakness in the face of motivated, implacable foes.

On 10 September the Bush administration was facing flak for pressing for oil drilling in Alaska. September 11 was a classic 'event', of a kind even Macmillan's worst nightmares couldn't conjure up. Before September 11, the Bush administration had been happily pursuing business relations with the Taliban. Before September 11, Saddam Hussein was an irritant. Suddenly, the world changed. The Taliban were harbouring an international terrorist mastermind, and Saddam Hussein was developing weapons of mass destruction, an imminent threat to the west. Checkmate, Adrian. Game, Mike?

Unfortunately, nothing is quite so simple.

When the Bush administration decided that 9/11 was the work of al-Qaeda (a group America had helped finance when it wanted the Soviets beaten up in Afghanistan), they decided to go after its head, a renegade Saudi millionaire called Osama bin Laden. A man based, according to their best intelligence, in Afghanistan. The Pentagon didn't even have plans to attack Afghanistan. But if the military had trouble pointing to it on a map, the Bush team didn't. Afghanistan sat between one of the biggest new supplies of oil in the world, the Caspian, and one of the biggest new markets, India and Pakistan. September 11, like the Burnhams' kidnapping, might have been an event out of the blue, but the players of the grand chessboard could certainly use it to their advantage.

Zbigniew Brzezinski, strategic adviser to several US presidents and one of Washington's pre-eminent geo-political gurus, believes Eurasia has been the centre of world power since the continents started interacting some 500 years ago.

Whaddaya know?

I cannot think of a time when we have had a region emerge as suddenly to become as strategically significant as the Caspian.

US Vice-President Dick Cheney in 1998, then a consultant on oil pipelines to central Asian countries

His thinking, echoing Lord Curzon, is summed up in a book long on politics, short on laughs, called *The Grand Chessboard: American Primacy and its Geostrategic Imperatives*. It's *the* book if you play world politics like chess and, according to Adrian's chessboard theory, that is just how they play it in the powerful corners of Washington.

There may be no checkmate in global chess but there are rules. Control of resources is rule number one. America's security relies on the guarantee of a supply of cheap, plentiful oil. That means controlling the Middle East, where the largest supplies of oil currently reside, and Eurasia, where large supplies are waiting to come online. This view of the world says that dominance of central Asia will ensure not only new sources of energy and mineral wealth, but also a guard-post over American control of the oil reserves of the Middle East. Remarkably, Brzezinski's book reads like the *Civilization User's Guide*:

> The three grand imperatives of imperial geo-strategy are to prevent collusion and maintain security dependence among the vassals, to keep tributaries pliant and protected, and to keep the barbarians from coming together.

The Romans couldn't have put it better.

Right in the middle of Eurasia sits the Caspian Sea, packed full of oil. Pipelines from the Caspian must travel through neighbouring countries—specifically through Russia (a friend of the US, but not a trusted one), Iran (labelled a member of the 'axis of evil' by George W. Bush, and suspected nuclear rebel), or (to get to Pakistan or India) . . . wait for it . . . Afghanistan.

Forget events, we're back to the chessboard.

Despite America's immediate fingering of Afghanistan, it wasn't the most obvious culprit of the 9/11 crimes. None of the September 11 hijackers were Afghans (or Iraqis, for that matter). On the contrary, fifteen of the nineteen hijackers were Saudis. But, inconveniently for the chess players, Saudi Arabia is the spiritual home of Islam, is immensely rich, has the world's

> It was easier to conquer it [the East] than to know what to
> do with it.
>
> Sir Horace Walpole, March 1772

biggest oil reserves, and at the time was also the Middle Eastern home of American soldiers and airmen. The events of 9/11 put the superpower into a compromising position: the connections between Saudi Arabia and the terrorist events were clear, but the US could not blame a friend and ally in a volatile region. When the US House–Senate Intelligence Committee released its 900-page report on the attacks in July 2003, the 28-page section on Saudi Arabia had been removed. It was classified.

America decided it didn't have to get heavy with the Saudis at that stage: for the grandmasters of world chess, the fact that Saudi renegade Osama bin Laden was holed up in Afghanistan after the 9/11 attacks was a gift. The fundamentalist Muslim Taliban government in Afghanistan had already annoyed the US government because it wouldn't do as it was told. It couldn't be trusted to allow a valuable oil pipeline through its state. So a war instigated by a renegade ally took US troops to Afghanistan, the Philippines and Iraq. The 'war on terror' suddenly had a logic. Secure resources. Establish bases. Strike out. Maintain the disparity. Forget events, dear boy. Security is a chess player's game.

Non-events

Revealingly, it is more difficult to find evidence to support the events theory—but it can be done. The key to understanding events lies with the concept of democracy. If America and its allies stand for anything, says this point of view, it is freedom— the right to pursue your own dream, whatever that dream might be, and the energy, vitality and growth that freedom brings to the world as a whole. Democracy protects people's right not to be told what to do by the state. If we don't like what they are up to, we can kick out the chess playing elite through elections.

So America must pursue the cause of democracy, not only in the protection of its own people's rights to democracy, but also, pre-emptively, wherever freedom is threatened by outside interests. By attacking states that provide succour to terror, America is protecting the free world from its enemies. It is making the world secure for us to pursue our individual dreams. By attacking al-Qaeda in Afghanistan, Saddam Hussein in Iraq, the gangsters of the southern Philippines and, as the twenty-first century progresses, whoever else looks dangerous to American interests, America is rightfully defending the security and freedom of everyone who shares its values of freedom and justice.

Harvard professor Samuel Huntington, the author of *Clash of Civilizations* and whose name (along with Francis Fukuyama's—see 'Democracy') invariably surfaces whenever big geo-political issues are discussed, comes down on Mike's side of the argument:

> A world without US primacy will be a world with more violence and disorder and less democracy and economic growth than a world where the United States continues to have more influence than any other country in shaping global affairs. The sustained international primacy of the United States is central to the welfare and security of Americans and to the future of freedom, democracy, open economies and international order in the world.

Of course, the challenge for Mr Huntington's political acolytes, such as Mr Cheney and Mr Bush, is communicating the good they are bringing the world over the sound of the TV news announcing the accidental bombing of an Afghan wedding party, or the progress of an Iraqi child amputee. Many devotees of the chessboard theory point out that, since the media is owned by members of the power elite, it is all too easy to drown out the tragic consequences of their heinous actions under Orwell's diet of sport, crime and astrology, not to mention sex and 'Big Brother'-style reality TV.

Whether the press is free or not, the images of destroyed lives do make it through the noise, and we inevitably ask whether our ends justify our brutal means. It is certainly enough to make you question the motivations of our leaders. The complexities of governing a sprawling and threatened empire have been common to governors since the dawn of time. Plato's solution was to create a group of 'philosopher-kings': 'The ruling class in a just society should be men apprenticed to the art of ruling, drawn from the rational and wise, bred from the finest families'. 'Government,' he said, 'was a special art in which competence, as in any other profession, could be acquired only by study.' Strangely enough, we have more students of government these days but few, if any, philosopher-kings.

> The philosophers must become kings in our cities or those who are now kings and potentates must learn to seek wisdom like true philosophers, and so political power and intellectual wisdom will be joined in one. Until that day, there can be no rest from the troubles for the cities, and I think for the whole human race.
>
> Plato

We needn't feel too bad if our leaders don't match up to Platonic ideals. The greatest minds of the twentieth century grappled with this issue in vain. In 1932, physicist Albert Einstein wrote to psychologist Sigmund Freud lamenting the inability of the world's finest minds to influence the course of world affairs, and asked him how intellectuals could work towards peace. Einstein revealed himself to be a confirmed adherent of the chessboard theory. He thought that those who crave power are hostile to any notion that would limit national sovereignty, and a 'small but determined group' who benefit financially from war supports them in this. They regard warfare 'simply as an occasion to advance their personal interests and enlarge their personal authority'. He asked Freud how he thought it was that men are aroused so easily into hatred, 'even to sacrifice their lives'? And, more ambitiously, 'Is it possible to control man's mental evolution so as to make him proof against the psychosis of hate and destructiveness?'

Freud's response? . . . don't hold your breath: 'Conflicts of interest between man and man are resolved, in principle, by recourse to violence.' He wrote that even the law is a form of violence, 'the suppression of brute force by the transfer of power to a larger combination, founded on the community of sentiments linking up its members'. Men are brutal victims of their urges, Freud believed, urges of love and urges of hate, of conservation and unification versus destruction and murder. His solution: a superior class of independent thinkers, unamenable to intimidation and fervent in the quest for truth, whose function it would be to guide the masses dependent on their lead. There is no need to point out how little the rule of politicians and the Church's ban on liberty of thought encourage such a new creation. The ideal conditions would obviously be found in a community where every man subordinated his instinctive life to the dictates of reason.

Well, the world isn't run from a university campus yet, and you don't hear a lot of public debate suggesting that it should be. As for 'reason', one solid lesson Freud's own century has left us with is the inadequacy of reason as the sole compass for

> Reason is only reason, and satisfies man's reasoning capacity, while wanting is a manifestation of the whole of life—that is the whole of human life, including reason and various little itches.
>
> Fyodor Dostoyevsky, *Notes from the Underground*

our affairs. We have seen that in using reason humanity can justify anything, from genocide to global warming. Reason is too blunt a tool for humanity, in Crunch Time as in any time that has come before.

Can Mike and Adrian agree?

Oddly enough we can. We can agree on what to do.

In the end what matters for you and me is not whether we live in a world that's at the mercy of events, or a giant chessboard. What matters is how we should behave. Remember Blaise Pascal (from the 'Science' chapter) and his conundrum about the existence of God? Pascal decided that it was better to behave as if God existed and be wrong, than to behave as if he didn't and be wrong. Chessboards and events may be simplistic ways of looking at the world, but they do give some insight into how *we* ought to behave. Should we act differently if we are living in a world governed by chess rules or one governed by events? The answer is no. Surely it is better to behave as if we are living in a chessboard world and be wrong than to behave as if we live in an events world and be wrong?

First and foremost, the stark difference between the two ends of the spectrum emphasises the fact that we have a duty to scepticism. When the crunch comes it is our responsibility to question, examine, interrogate and judge the motivations of those in power. More than that, as we saw in 'Democracy', we should be acting to influence them.

Modernity has made ignorance easy. We are fed opinions and news and told that if we vote every four years or so we have exercised our democratic duty. But 'Democracy' showed that democracy and a free press are chimeras, excuses for silence and self-satisfaction. If we are to hand the world over to our children with a clear conscience then surely we have a duty to find out the closest version of the 'truth' there is, and to act.

The world may be a crazy, unconnected place, as our leaders would have us believe, in which progress towards dignity for all is made haltingly and with fiendish trade-offs. But even if it is, we still have a duty to be sceptical, because power is as power does. We have to assume that people in high office, whether of good intention or not, are generally lazy and greedy or at the very least lacking crucial information. They are people like us, not philosopher-kings making stabs in the dark and choices based on their best interests and those of their immediate circle, or what they believe is in ours.

Things look even uglier under the chessboard theory. If the endpoint of our civilisation is a world where the ruling elite wields power as if it was a God-given right, destroying competitors and grinding the peoples of other states almost randomly into the ground, then we the people are at fault for allowing it to happen. This point of view entails important responsibilities for us as individuals, living with the consequences of the great game of civilisation. We must understand how crucial our freedoms are to what it means to be a person at the beginning of the twenty-first century, because it is only those freedoms that can protect the world against the ravages of overweening power.

We must act in the certainty that fundamentally our civilisation is based on the twin concepts of freedom and understanding. Our societies draw their vitality from our freedom to fulfil our own potential or not, to move freely without answering to anyone, to associate and speak as we wish. But equally important is the responsibility that entails us to understand the impact of our actions on others.

Freedom and understanding—these are the foundation of our civilisation. These two concepts are a constant, no matter what type of world we are living in. Just as important is our ability to translate it into everyday action, into the causes that we support, into political activism, into what we teach our children, into how we relate to our employers, into where we put our energy—in our work, our relationships—and into what

In Bush's America post 9/11:

- the FBI can spy on groups without any evidence of wrongdoing
- the FBI can spy on people for a year without evidence of wrong-doing, up from 30 days
- the US Customs Service can open outbound international mail without a warrant
- the US Attorney-General can lock up non-citizens indefinitely purely on the basis of suspicion
- 'nonlawful combatants' are denied most of the trial rights granted to soldiers and civilians.

Source: ACLU

The Australian Security Intelligence Organisation Legislation Amendment (Terrorism) Act 2002:

- allows ASIO to arrest and hold people incommunicado and without legal representation for 48 hours
- reverses the burden of proof—suspects must prove themselves innocent
- restricts access to public documents and removes protection from journalists who protect their sources.

In the UK:

- laws introduced since September 11 include the Anti-Terrorism, Crime and Security Act 2001
- laws introduced allow the government to detain foreigners indef-initely without trial
- the Civil Contingencies Act allows British Government Minis-ters to override acts of parliament in the case of an 'emergency'.

we buy and consume. Awareness is all, and it has critical links to almost everything we do.

George Kennan ended his 'Long Telegram' with these words:

Finally, we must have courage and self-confidence to cling to our own methods and conceptions of human society. After all, the

> greatest danger that can befall us in coping with this problem of
> Soviet communism is that we shall allow ourselves to become
> like those with whom we are coping.

He was writing for a different set of leaders, but the message is one that ours should always be forced to heed.

If September 11 opened our eyes to the big bad world outside, it has also opened them to the fragility of our comfortable existences. In the twenty-first century, scepticism must become a core competence. On 12 September 2001, we suddenly matured enough to understand that the motives of the terrorists and states who would destroy us, and the governments who would protect us, are not black or white, but an uncomfortable combination of both.

Pawn sacrifice—the fate of the Burnhams

A little over a year after their capture, and a few days after their nineteenth wedding anniversary, the Burnhams were caught up in a desperate firefight. Martin was shot and killed. Gracia Burnham, the only survivor, was badly wounded. But the Filipino military was happy. The troops had killed Abu Sabaya, although with no dead body to be found they had to make do with waving his captured Oakleys about like 'movie Indians' claiming a scalp. That was the tragic end to the Burnhams' weekend in paradise.

The sad truth about this story is that while resorts like Dos Palmas can be found wherever there's blue ocean, white sand and a palm tree, they are not insulated from the people who live there and the problems that lie just a speedboat ride away. The international luxury tourist experience had lost in a face-off with real life. For these innocents, events lost out to the chessboard.

Making the world's exotic holiday destinations safe isn't precisely why we hand over our tax dollars. But for most of us it's the nearest we come to connecting with the Realpolitik of international security. For the real players in the grand geo-political chess game, there are more immediate concerns than the spread of freedom and democracy. American hostages make for poor publicity, but for the president of the US and his men the Burnhams' lives weren't as crucial to underpinning America's power in the Pacific as ensuring access to military bases. Offering a helping hand to a Philippine administration that was sympathetic to US interests, the most it had been in a decade, was simply irresistible. Martin Burnham's life wasn't even a fraction of a factor in the great game of civilisation. The game—the global trade in weaponry, cash and influence—carries on regardless of our vacation requirements.

For us, sitting outside the games room, scepticism, freedom and understanding is where we start and end. It is the source of our societies' vitality, innovation and growth—economic or otherwise. Security relies on assumptions which, when looked at closely, often turn out to be false.

Martin Burnham, caught up in the great game and held captive in the Philippine jungle, had a particular perspective on what his life was all about. Whether you agree with his brand of Christianity or not, you have to admire his courage, fortitude and sense of mission. 'We might not leave this jungle alive,' he said, in his final television broadcast, 'but at least we can leave this world serving the Lord. We can serve Him right here where we are, and with gladness.'

In this sceptical and secular world, it would be nice for everybody to have such a solidity of belief in something greater than themselves.

6
PEOPLE, PEOPLE, PEOPLE . . .

A business trip into the terrifying heart of America. Sitting next to Mike on the plane is a guy called Brian, with whom he strikes up a conversation. What was interesting about Brian was not his job as a salesman of locker systems to theme parks, but his reading matter. He was reading *The Death of the West* by US presidential hopeful and card-carrying member of the crackpot religious right, Pat Buchanan.

What interested Mike in his conversation with Brian was that Brian believed every word of it, and was terrified of the consequences of the seething mass of humanity waiting to invade his country.

It would have been easy to dismiss the book as ridiculous ratbag far-right nonsense, except that just at that time Australia's Prime Minister John Howard was having an international row over 438 Afghan boat people rescued from a sinking Indonesian fishing vessel by a Norwegian cargo ship, the *Tampa*. Rather than let these people land on Australian shores at Christmas Island, Howard ordered the Australian Special Forces to board the ship and take it to a remote South Pacific island. In the process he diplomatically alienated everyone from the Indonesian government, who he blamed for the refugees' presence in the South Seas, to the Norwegian

MASS IMMIGRATION

SKYROCKETING THIRD WORLD POPULATIONS

COLLAPSING BIRTH RATES IN THE WESTERN WORLD

A CULTURAL WAR DESTROYING AMERICA'S FREEDOM AND HERITAGE

What *The Death of the West* foretells is astonishing.

- Not a single European country has a birth rate that will enable it to survive in its present form through this century. By 2050, only one-tenth of the world's population will be Europeans, and it will be the oldest tenth on earth, with a median age of 50.
- Russia, already in a terminal population crisis, will by 2050 be driven out of Central Asia by Islamic invaders and lose huge slices of Siberia and her Far East to China, which is 15 times more populous.
- There are 30 million foreign-born in the US and between 9 and 11 million illegal aliens—as many illegals as there are people in Massachusetts, Rhode Island and Connecticut combined.
- America is losing the cultural war. Militant paganism is crowding the old faiths. Separatism is triumphing over integration. The melting pot has become a salad bowl. And the impact upon American society, politics and culture will be devastating.

In an even-handed, thoughtful tone, Patrick J. Buchanan documents the sea changes that have already begun to take place in our society. *The Death of the West* is a timely, provocative book that asks a question (on the back cover) that quietly troubles millions: Is the America we grew up in gone forever?

government, who he blamed for the cargo ship's presence in the South Seas.

Meanwhile, in Europe, headlines were being dominated by a bunch of young, male Middle Eastern refugees camped by the Channel Tunnel. These refugees, if that is what they were, were making nightly forays to try to jump on trains or walk through the tunnel to get to the UK. They refused to file for asylum until they hit the UK because that country's asylum laws are more liberal than those in continental Europe, meaning they stand a better chance of not getting sent back home if they make it to Britain. In response the British government was bitching at the French government, saying it wasn't doing enough about this mob. The French government was pointing the finger at Britain, blaming its liberal policies for attracting the rabble through France in the first place.

Mike picked up a copy of the Buchanan book in a bookshop and sent it to Adrian.

————Original message————
From: Adrian
To: Mike
Subject: Book
Ah . . . thanks for the book.
Why?

————Original message————
From: Mike
To: Adrian
Subject: Re: Book
It's the seething masses.

————Original message————
From: Adrian
To: Mike
Subject: Re: Re: Book
It's the Huns.

As Adrian pointed out, this is hardly the first time hordes of uninvited aliens have threatened a 'great' civilisation.

Barbarians at the gate

In the second half of the fourth century a nomadic people from central Asia began heading west. They were the Huns—archers and horsemen, possibly from Korea originally. Whatever their reasons for leaving their homeland steppes and pastures they kept going, decade after decade until they reached the edges of Europe. History is silent about their progress until they reached the borders of the world known to the Western Roman Empire. By the 370s they had reached the area between the Dniester and Dnieper rivers in what is now the Ukraine. There they ran into a people called the Greuthingi, who they defeated and enslaved.

A little later they began pressing at the Greuthingi's neighbours, the Tervingi, sacking their settlements, raping and pillaging their way along the Empire's great river boundary, the Danube. The Tervingi's leader, Fritigern, sent a diplomatic mission to the Roman Emperor Valens, asking for help. It was headed by a missionary bishop called Ulfila, known by contemporaries as 'the Moses of our time' because he'd previously led persecuted Christians out of the Tervingi's clutches and into the safety of Empire. Against the superior military power of the Hun, the Tervingi wanted asylum status for their entire people under the protection of Rome. The Emperor reluctantly granted permission to Fritigern to lead his people across the Danube and settle in the Empire *en masse*. Tens of thousands of people and their possessions entered Western Europe as immigrants.

By all accounts, benefits and social services for the new-comers were a little thin on the ground. The Romans, according to the great historian Edward Gibbon:

> levied an ungenerous and oppressive tax on the wants of the hungry barbarians. The vilest food was sold at an extravagant price and . . . the markets were filled with the flesh of dogs and unclean animals who had died of disease.

Tired, poor, hungry and miserable, Fritigern's people turned on the Empire. At Adrianople, on what today is Turkey's European border, his refugee army routed and butchered Valens and his Roman legions. Fritigern's successor took the refugees to Rome, where they sacked the city and started the process we know as the decline and fall of the Roman Empire.

Fritigern's people are better known as the Goths. Just like the hordes of central Asians camped outside the Channel Tunnel, the Goths arrived in the Empire as immigrants. They were the enemy at the gate, waiting for an opportunity to turn on their hosts and masters and bring down the glory of civilisation. Pat Buchanan and John Howard's worst nightmare. Yikes.

Our Crunch Time hordes

Let's be clear about this: we live in a divided world. On one side of the line sit the 'golden' billion, those lucky enough to be born in the 'rich' world. On the other side of the line sit the, ah, 'tin' five billion, who are born in the 'poor' world.

The line that separates these two global constituencies is dotted. Millions of people try and cross it every year. Some succeed, some die, some get sent to hellish prisons on Pacific islands by the Australian government, others get sent to hellish housing estates in Glasgow by the British government, others aren't so lucky—they get sent home.

What becomes of the surplus of human life? It is either, 1st. destroyed by infanticide, as among the Chinese and Lacedemonians; or 2d. it is stifled or starved, as among other nations whose population is commensurate to its food; or 3d. it is consumed by wars and endemic diseases; or 4th. it overflows, by emigration, to places where a surplus of food is attainable.

James Madison, writing in 1791

Those of us born into the golden billion stand half a chance of living a long life in relative comfort, meeting and exceeding our need for calories, warmth and even entertainment. Those born into the tin five billion stand a good chance of never meeting any of those requirements. As we shall see in chapter 8, globalisation is making a winner-take-all world. At the beginning of the twenty-first century, the richest 15 per cent of the world divides amongst itself almost 80 per cent of the world's wealth, while the poorest half of the world gets by on just over 1 per cent.

This gap, between those who clearly could afford to worry less about their standard of living and those who don't know what standard of living means, got bigger during the last century. In 1870 the world's richest countries, Britain and the United States, had incomes per head roughly nine times larger than the poorest countries. In 2002 that number had shot up to 225. The World Bank calculates that the average income in the world's richest 20 countries is 37 times the average in the poorest 20, and the gap doubled in the last four decades of the twentieth century.

The UN figures that nearly half the world's population, 2.8 billion, live on less than US$2 per day. Asylum seekers may not know exactly what lies in store for them on the other side of that dotted line, but their economic decision-making skills are as rational as you can get. On the rich side of the line, even the cows earn more: each cow in Europe receives US$2.20 a day from the taxpayer in subsidies and other handouts, while in Japan cows make an even better living, US$7.50 a day. Apart from sore udders and a date with a dinner plate, the economic logic is inescapable.

But these are just numbers. To say, for example, that 1.2 billion people live on less than $1 a day is one thing, to understand what those lives are like is another. $1 a day is what the World Bank calls 'absolute poverty'. It means 'malnutrition, illiteracy, disease, squalid surroundings, high infant mortality and low life expectancy'. More ugly statistics: of the world's 1.2 billion absolute poor, the World Bank says two thirds are underfed and the same number illiterate, and almost all are drinking dirty water with no access to even the most basic sanitation. In rich countries, less than one child in a hundred dies before the age of five, in poor countries it's twenty times that amount: 30 000 kids die each day from preventable causes. Average life expectancy in rich countries is around 80; in sub-Saharan Africa it's around 50. To be poor today is to live a nastier, more brutish and shorter life.

Meanwhile, *Forbes* magazine announced in September 2003 that the net worth of the 400 richest people in the US has gone up by ten per cent to nearly US$1 trillion. The three richest—Bill Gates, Warren Buffett and Paul Allen—have assets that exceed the combined gross national products of 600 million people (that works out at a couple of hundred million people each) living in 49 of the world's poorest countries.

When the people aboard the *Tampa* or in the Calais Red Cross camps consider whether they ought to leave their homes, lives and families and undertake life threateningly treacherous voyages in an attempt to cross that line, they are acting on the human impulse to improve the hand they were dealt at birth. Experts at the Rand think-tank in the US believe migrants who score a green card letting them into the country increase their lifetime earnings by about US$300 000. Not too far off a modest win on the lottery.

It's no mystery why Mr Buchanan, Mr Howard and, more to the point, the people who give them their support and vote them into office behave as if they are in a war with the barbarian hordes. They are.

In this age of globalisation, information may flow freely around the world, capital sloshes in bucket loads around the globe, goods and services too, but people do not. Politicians like Pat Buchanan and John Howard play to their people's fear of 'being swamped' (to use the words of Britain's Home Affairs

Minister) by the unwashed hordes on the other side of the dotted line. And the situation is not going to get any better.

The winner's curse

For most species, evolutionary success is measured in sheer numbers. If a particular type of fly or baboon is successful against predators, if it is good at finding food and water, surviving weather and natural disasters and at defeating disease, its numbers will grow. By this strictly biological definition, *Homo sapiens* has been immensely successful, particularly throughout the twentieth century. Despite two world wars, genocides, persecution and conflict, the number of people on the face of the earth grew from around 1.6 billion in 1900 to more than 6 billion in 2000—nearly a fourfold increase. When we passed the 6 billion mark (on or around 12 October 1999 say demographers), *Homo sapiens* had already exceeded the biomass—the sheer bulk—of any large animal species that ever existed on the land.

World population growth through history

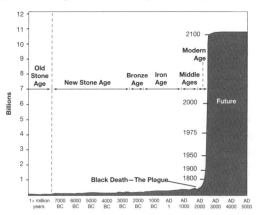

Source: Population Reference Bureau; and United Nations, *World Population Projections to 2100* (1998).

We win.

There is, however, a noisy bunch of people who think this is a bit simplistic. They reckon the human race is too successful for its own good. Their argument goes like this.

As we saw in 'Environment', the world's 6 billion people are already chewing up the earth faster than they can repay the debt. The scientists who measure these things think we passed the point where we were using all the resources that nature could replenish back in 1978. Ever since then we've been draining the tank, exhausting fisheries, fossil fuels, water supplies. The lot.

Some scientists believe that, if we are all to have European standards of living and enough food and water to go around, the earth can sustain only about 2 billion people. So the question becomes, who's jumping off, you or me? For the rich world politicians and their constituencies, the answer is clear: them, not us.

Looking at this all-too-easy-to-paint picture of doom and gloom, there is at least one figure from history who would sport a wry smile.

Too many people, not enough food

In Europe at the end of the eighteenth century, the civilised world of dinner parties, gentlemen's clubs and genteel philosophy was agog with the possibilities afforded by the French

---

What if the 1.3 billion Chinese partied like Americans?

- They would need more paper each year than the world currently produces.
- They would need 100 million tons of seafood every year—the entire world fish catch.
- They would need over 80 million barrels of oil a day—slightly more than the 74 million barrels per day the world now produces.

Revolution. Here, it seemed, was a blazing example of a modern democratic politics in action. Utopia here we come. French-style democracy would take the world to the next level of civilisation, in which people conducted politics in a civilised manner without resorting to violence, a social order that could provide everyone with opportunity and sustenance.

In France, for instance, the Marquis de Condorcet, a liberal aristocrat, wrote an essay arguing that human progress unfolded naturally in a series of ten stages, the ninth ending with the founding of the French Republic, the tenth and last being a world of equality in wealth, gender and opportunity and, crucially, of abundance. Condorcet was not alone in his optimism. Others picked up the revolutionary theme and ran with it. In England, for instance, best-selling writer and journalist William Godwin (the poet Percey Shelley's father-in-law) wrote 'Of Avarice and Profusion' about the forthcoming society of equality, peace, brotherhood, happiness and altruism.

If the early twenty-first century feels like Crunch Time for the writers and readers of this book, so too did the end of the eighteenth century for those living in that age. For progressives like Condorcet and Godwin a new era was dawning. Conservatives, on the other hand, were frightened by the signs of social chaos and decay they saw all around them and the spectre of social collapse. According to one of the most influential of their number:

> The great and unlooked for discoveries that have taken place of late years in natural philosophy, the increasing diffusion of general knowledge from the extension of the art of printing, the ardent and unshackled spirit of inquiry that prevails throughout the lettered and even unlettered world, the new and extraordinary lights that have been thrown on political subjects which dazzle and astonish the understanding, and particularly that tremendous phenomenon in the political horizon, the French Revolution, which, like a blazing comet, seems destined either to inspire with fresh life and vigour, or to scorch up and destroy the shrinking inhabitants of the earth, have all concurred to lead

many able men into the opinion that we were touching on a period big with the most important changes, changes that would in some measure be decisive of the future fate of mankind.

This philosopher was Thomas Malthus—briefly mentioned in 'Environment'—an English cleric who sat down to write out his thoughts, following a conversation with a friend, about 'the general question of the future improvement of society', and ended up kicking off a centuries-long feud about the nature of human society.

Malthus was a pillar of England's conservative establishment and the ideas of Condorcet and Godwin about the future of society were pouring intellectual gasoline over everything he stood for. His answer was the none-too-snappily titled *Essay on the Principle of Population, as it affects the Future Improvement of Society with Remarks on the Speculations of Mr. Godwin, M. Condorcet, and other Writers.*

Malthus opened with a couple of concepts that he felt were a given: first, that food is necessary to the existence of man; second, that the passion between the sexes is necessary and will remain nearly in its present state. Reasonable enough, perhaps. He then went on to draw a conclusion which has shaped the nature of the population debate ever since:

> The power of population is indefinitely greater than the power in the earth to produce subsistence for man.
>
> Population, when unchecked, increases in a geometrical (1, 2, 4, 8 . . .) ratio. Subsistence increases only in an arithmetical (1, 2, 3, 4 . . .) ratio. A slight acquaintance with numbers will show the immensity of the first power in comparison to the

---

The view which I have given of human life has a melancholy hue, but I feel conscious that I have drawn these dark tints from a conviction that they are really in the picture, and not from a jaundiced eye or an inherent spleen of disposition.

Thomas Malthus

second. This implies a strong and constantly operating check on
population from the difficulty of subsistence.

Malthus wrote that as a result, French Revolution or not,
mankind was destined to be caught in a struggle between a
human population continually trying to expand and a world
unable to feed it. Additional checks on human population
would be provided by war, disease, poverty, famine and crime.
Malthus parachuted himself into instant celebrity with these
gloomy assertions when he published his essay in 1798. Ever
since he's been reviled or praised, but never ignored, by all sides
in the population debate, and his thinking bent to all sorts of
purposes.

Doomsayers reckon Malthus day will soon be with us. In
the 1960s and 1970s, a rash of ultra-Malthusian books announced that explosive population growth would soon overwhelm
the earth's ability to feed its people. Disaster was imminent. In
1968, biologist Paul Ehrlich published *The Population Bomb*. If
the title gave a pretty good idea of which way Ehrlich thought
things were headed, his opening made it crystal clear:

> The battle to feed all humanity is over. In the 1970s and 80s
> hundreds of millions of people will starve to death in spite of any
> crash programmes embarked upon now.

At the same time, ecologist Garret Hardin famously quoted
the lesson of the tragedy of the commons we mentioned in
'Environment':

> Ruin is the destination toward which all men rush, each pursuing
> his own best interest in a society that believes in the freedom of
> the commons.

In a 1968 essay he applied it to population growth and its
effects on the earth's finite resources. He argued that you need
to combine political and social theory with biological data:

> A finite world can support only a finite population: therefore,
> population growth must eventually equal zero.

Like Ehrlich he'd seen the future and come to tell us it sucked.
Hardin wanted rigorous regulation of the human population—
'Freedom to breed will bring ruin to all.'

In the 1990s Paul Hawken wrote in *The Ecology of Commerce*:

> People are breeding exponentially. The process of fulfilling their
> wants and needs is stripping the earth of its biotic capacity to
> produce life; a climactic burst of consumption by a single species
> is overwhelming the skies, earth, water and fauna.

Other books and articles followed the same line, with titles like
Born to Starve and *The Ostrich Factor*; academics and commentators warned that feeding the masses was going to be
impossible. Each of these invoked the ghost of Malthus, saying
that after centuries of growth the impending disaster repre-
sented by the population boom of the late twentieth century
was the old vicar come to life.

They couldn't have been more wrong. According to the
United Nations Food and Agriculture Organization, the number
of hungry people in the developing world dropped from
920 million in 1980 to 799 million twenty years later, even
though the world's population grew by 1.6 billion in that time.
Somewhere in the region of 25 million people starved to death
in the two decades since Ehrlich wrote his book. Nothing for
the world to be proud of, but far from the hundreds of millions
Ehrlich predicted.

This gives powerful fuel to the population optimists, who
point at the doomsters' predictions and laugh. Look at the vast
growth in human population over the 200 years since Malthus
was writing. They say that we have managed all right so far,
and there is no reason to think we might not manage so well in
the future. The human race, they like to point out, has been
quite successful producing enough food for its growing needs

for the 200 years since Malthus was around. And most of this success has been due to our newfound ability to grow more food from the same amount of land, through mechanisations, fertilisers, weedkillers, crop rotations, new seed varieties and all of the other great things we have learned in the agricultural revolution of the last two centuries.

People like Buchanan, however, believe the pendulum is swinging Malthus' way again, and it's Africa where the Reverend's logic is being revived. Between 1995 and 2000 cereal production in sub-Saharan Africa went up by 4 million tonnes to 73 million (17 per cent). The number of people living there went up by 76 million to 653 million (just 12 per cent). Back in 1995 that worked out at 330 grams of cereal per person, per day—that's eleven bowls of breakfast cereal each. In just five years that was down to ten cereal bowls. Thomas Malthus may well wink down through history: 'Don't say I didn't tell you so.'

As African children go hungry, in the rich world most people have forgotten what it's like to be really hungry (beyond the odd carbohydrate craving). In fact, the rich world is suffering badly from the opposite problem—we're too fat. Lazy lifestyles and overeating are the biggest causes of serious health problems. According to the World Health Organization, this accounts for the deaths of 2 million people a year across the

Rich man, poor man

	Per cent consumed	
	by people in industrialised countries	by poorest 20% in developing countries
Total energy resources	58	< 4
Meat and fish	45	5
Paper	84	< 1
Vehicles	87	< 1
Telephone lines	74	1.5

Source: United Nations Populations Fund.

world. It is the main cause of the world's biggest killer (more than AIDS, malaria or war)—heart disease. It is also the principle risk factor in diabetes, and is heavily implicated in cancer and other diseases. In just five years, between 1995 and 2000, the number of clinically obese people in the world ballooned to 300 million, over a third of whom are thought to be suffering from weight-related health problems. We did say that we live in a divided world, didn't we?

The numbers game

Every second, five people are born and two people die, a net gain of three human beings. At this rate the world's population should double every 40 years. So by the end of the century there would be 36 billion of us, which would be a squeeze. But actually the rate is slowing down. The UN reckons that the world's current population of 6 billion will, by 2050, be between 7 and 14 billion—best guess, around 9. Then, perhaps, it will peak, tail off, fall, or maybe stabilise.

The statistics buffs who model these things call this process 'demographic transition'. It starts with people living longer lives—as society provides better health care, hygiene and nutrition, death rates go down. For a while, birth rates stay high

---

The global population has doubled in the last 40 years

When Adrian was born there were 3 202 830 000 people on earth. It has increased by 97 per cent since then.

When Mike was born there were 3 475 852 000 people on earth. And it's increased by 82 per cent since then.

Source: Musee de l'Homme, Paris, France
<http://www-popexpo. ined.fr/eMain.html>

while death rates fall, causing a baby boom. But eventually social pressures shrink the birth rate back down and the population stabilises again. Birth control, greater freedom of choice for women, and the ability of parents to invest more in fewer children mean smaller families. This pretty much describes what's happened in Europe during the three centuries of the industrial revolution.

The 'demographic transition' has speeded up in developing countries, especially East Asia, where it's been telescoped into decades rather than centuries as it was in Europe. After galloping expansion (700 million more Chinese have joined the world since the 1950s) countries such as China and South Korea have halved their population growth rates in the past two decades. In India, however, fertility rates are still high, and in Pakistan they're the highest in Asia. Africa below the Sahara desert, where food shortage concerns are growing, has phenomenally high population growth rates. Here, improvements in health care and hygiene have raised life expectancy a bit, but three quarters of Africa's population lives on the land so there is little incentive for them to reduce family sizes—in many African countries average families still have six or more children. In Kenya in recent years there have been four times as many births as deaths.

Population changes take a lifetime to filter through. People born today will have children some 20 to 40 years from now,

---

Dinner party factlets

- Global population is growing but that growth is slowing down.
- The average woman had 4.3 kids in 1960, but only 2.6 in 2000.
- To stop numbers rising, the average would have to drop to 2.1— the 'replacement rate'.
- Population worrier Paul Ehrlich had a vasectomy to prove he meant business.

The five most fecund countries

Average number of kids per woman, 2000:

1 Niger	8.0
2 Yemen	7.6
3 Somalia	7.25
4 Angola	7.2
5 Uganda	7.1

Source: Economist Pocket World in figures, 2003.

List five countries that could really use less people, not more.

and with new technology possibly longer than that. So, if a country's birth rates peak now and then start to decline, women born today will still be fertile and having kids until the 2040s. And if we continue to live longer the delay will only get longer. Italy's birth rate is just 1.2, but the actual population will barely fall by a few million until well into the century. In the meantime, the population balance will shift, countries will get more older people and there'll be fewer youngsters.

Those shrinking population blues

Catholic Italy, as we mentioned above, has an extremely low birth rate, the second lowest in the world. It's so low that in 2002, in an historic address to the country's legislature, Pope John Paul II begged Italians to have more kids. But the lowest birth rate in the world belongs not to the Italians, but to their fellow Europeans and Roman Catholics, the Spanish, with just 1.15 births per woman. Spanish politicians of all persuasions are worried. Generally middle-aged and heading towards retirement, they can see a problem coming: who is going to pay their pensions? Low birth rates mean a shrinking labour force and a smaller tax base from which to fund social services, including pensions. Demographers predict that by 2050 Spain will have the world's highest percentage of the elderly—44 per cent of Spaniards will be over 60.

So why aren't Spanish women having kids? Academics say it's all down to women's greater contraceptive and life choices, along with more women choosing to delay childbirth, limit family size or remain childless. But this is not what Spain's women say. According to a survey by the Spanish Institute of Statistics, nearly a third of Spanish women of childbearing age want more *niños*. Asked why they don't have them, Spanish women give different reasons:

- high cost of living
- high female unemployment
- low pay and job insecurity
- employer hostility to maternity
- lack of affordable, accessible and high-quality childcare.

That's the 'rich' world for you. Politicians, though, aren't too bothered by these things. Their solution is more blunt—they're offering a cash bonus to women who have a third child. In Australia, families get $3000 for each new baby. But state bonuses for babies haven't worked in Singapore or Japan.

There is another solution for a country whose southern tip lies just twelve miles from Africa, but it is the spectre of this which terrifies the country's leaders: immigration. Spain has some of the strictest immigration laws in Europe—immigrants make up just 3.3 per cent of the Spanish population. Letting people in could fund the pensions and the social services. But, like John Howard and Pat Buchanan, Spaniards don't want to grow old in a country full of foreigners. They'll do anything other than let in the Goths.

Hell is other people

Which begs the question: what is it about foreigners that is so repugnant? Why is it that, since the time of the Roman Empire and before, people have been loyal to those who are born in their country and not to others? Human beings, it seems, are tribal—we feel loyalty most strongly towards those closest to us, and none towards strangers.

Just three months after September 11, Americans had dipped into their pockets to the tune of US$1.3 billion to support the people of lower Manhattan. This was an average of US$5300 per family, even though the people of lower Manhattan are among the wealthiest people in the country. Meanwhile, every day hundreds of millions of families in other parts of the world, affected by poverty, war and violence, go through equally harrowing experiences without a hope of anything like US$5300 compensation.

Why? Because, as we learnt in the 'Environment' chapter, it has only been about 10 000 years or 400 generations since we emerged from the primitive state of hunting, gathering and wandering the natural world to build communities, discover ways to mould the environment around us, and develop civil-isation. For most of those 10 000 years life has been a Darwinian struggle, a struggle against the elements, against other people also fighting to survive, against a world consistently working against us. We built strong defences against a brutal world, and the success of those defences ensured they were passed down the genetic line. In other words, we approach twenty-first century Crunch Time problems with a stone-age mentality.

It is this mentality that makes us consider those close to us more valuable to our evolutionary survival than others. It auto-matically means that those born on the other side of the dotted line less worthy. In the words of George W. Bush, 'first things first are the people who live in America'. This approach makes for simple, practical solutions to complex problems. Boat people

> We should all agree that each of us is bound to show kindness to his parents and spouse and children, and to other kinsmen in a less degree: and to those who may have rendered services to him, and any others whom he may have admitted to his intimacy and called friends: and to neighbours and fellow-countrymen more than others: and perhaps we may say to those of our own race more than to black or yellow men, and generally to human beings in proportion to their affinity to ourselves.
>
> Henry Sidgwick
> professor of moral philosophy at Cambridge University
> in *The Method of Ethics* (1874)

show up? Not our problem, shove them offshore again. Ethiopian famine? No mind, there are probably too many of them anyway. Unfortunately, Crunch Time problems are too complex for simple solutions; we cannot simply shove them offshore, because they have a way of coming back again, worse next time.

As we have seen throughout this book, things have changed, utterly, in only a few decades. There are billions more of us now than there were even when you were born, and there will be billions more very soon. While once we may have been able to argue that big global problems are not our concern, we no longer can. We need to find ways to live together.

What to do?

In 'Security', we saw how it didn't really matter whether events or a chessboard was the correct theory, because how we behave is unaffected. The same is true in the population debate. For your life and mine, it doesn't matter if neo-classical economic growth theory will help the least developed countries out of their predicament more efficiently than income redistribution.

It doesn't matter if economic growth, education or women's lib is the more effective way to convince poor women not to have too many children. It doesn't matter if free trade makes the world more prosperous than protectionism. It doesn't matter if genetically modified food will help feed the hungry mouths of the poor more efficiently, or whether it's an environmental nightmare. For the way we live our lives everyday, our goals in life and the values we ought to hold dear, it doesn't matter whether Malthus was wrong or right.

There are a few things that we do know.

- We know that unless there is a huge disaster in the not so distant future, there will be billions more people on the earth than there are now.
- We know that almost all those billions will be in the poor world.
- We know that the natural systems that support us, that enable us to grow food, supply water and provide the other things that make life worth living are under strain. In some parts of the world, they have already reached their limits. As the good Reverend Malthus would have it, population growth in these places is meeting resistance from social and environmental nasties. With continuing growth and pollution, many more places will seriously begin to bump up against Malthusian limits as well.
- We know that the more parts of the world that bump up against these limits, the nastier place the world, as a whole, will be. Places which hit their population limits cause all sorts of trouble: they spew out security threats, incubate diseases such as SARS and other new viruses, are the source of streams of refugees and migrants, and sap the energy and resources of the world as it tries to help.
- As the poor world gets nastier, so the rich world too becomes a scared and threatened place—putting up walls and barriers, pre-empting security threats by bombing the

hell out of poor and far-away countries, and conducting ugly, inhumane and obnoxious policies towards the tired, hungry and desperate that arrive on their doorsteps.

These are the things we know. From these facts, can we turn from the global and the macro, from the complex and insoluble, from the far away, hopeless and desperate to the up close and personal? Can we deduce from what we know the problems are what we ought to be doing about them?

At the Johannesburg Summit on Sustainable Development, the rich countries promised to put real resources behind the 'Millennium Development Goals' of cutting poverty, disease and environmental degradation. They agreed—Australia, the UK and the US among them—to:

> urge the developed countries that have not done so to make concrete efforts towards the target of 0.7% of GNP as official development assistance to developing countries.

This looks to be one of the emptiest promises ever made by the rich world to the poor. In 2002, only four countries in the world managed this seemingly painless objective: Denmark, The Netherlands, Norway and Sweden. The UK gave 0.32 per cent of its GDP as aid, Australia 0.25 per cent, while the richest and most dominant country of all, the US, gave a pitiful 0.1 per cent.

The US is some US$60 billion shy of its public commitment to the poor world, which seems like a lot. Until you

> At the moment, overseas development assistance is a bit over $50 billion, agricultural subsidies are $350 billion, and defense expenditures [are] somewhere between $900 billion and a trillion. So if you deal with the question of what I call the other war, $50 billion is probably not near enough.
>
> James Wolfensohn
> President of the World Bank

A quick lesson in international ethics from Peter Singer

Controversial ethicist Peter Singer uses the following example when he is talking to people about issues of international ethics:

> Imagine you were walking along and pass a shallow pond. Suddenly, a small child falls in and you realise that she is in danger of drowning. There is nobody else around. You could wade into the pond and save her, but that would get your suit wet, and ruin your new shoes, and you would be a bit late for your appointment because you would have to go home and change. Would you save the drowning girl? Clearly you would. If you walk on, clean, dry and on time, you would hardly be human.

Singer argues that the same is true of giving to charity. If you know that by giving, say, $200 to a poor world children's charity you could be fairly sure you were helping to save a child's life through inoculations, food or clean water, then surely by not doing so, and perhaps spending that money on a new jacket you really don't need, you are doing something equally grotesque. But because we are so busy in our lives we don't think about stuff like this, and poor children go on dying because of our (in) action.

realise that the country spends over a billion dollars a day on defence. And defence, after all, is simply what we call keeping the Goths outside the empire, the hordes on the other side of the dotted line. It is not too simplistic to say that using some of that money to make conditions on the other side of the dotted line more bearable might be a better way to achieve that objective.

In every chapter in this book we have seen how imbalances in the way that our societies conduct themselves are causing huge issues. In 'Money and work', 'Security', 'Science' and the rest, we've seen how Crunch Time values and lifestyles are causing Crunch Time issues. What has become clear as we have progressed through the future history of the twenty-first century is the seriousness of the problems the world now faces, and how much of it falls at our own feet.

'Whoa,' we hear our readers cry defensively, 'you can't lay this one at our feet. How is the massive growth in global population and poverty our problem? How on earth can anything we do help?'

Here, Malthus rides to the rescue. He said that human society is far from perfectible because there will never be enough to go around. But, as his critics will all too helpfully point out, we have become much, much better at squeezing more from less. We can now grow more food—healthily and sustainably—on the same piece of land, house more people comfortably in the same area, and use new techniques to learn to get more from one litre of water than we do at the moment. The world does have limits, but it is up to us how limited it is.

That is why it is Crunch Time . . . now. We can choose to senselessly barrel on into the future wasting and destroying the world around us and forcing those born on the other side of the line into ever more desperation. Or we can make the most out of what we have by recognising those limits and choosing modesty over extravagance.

We don't know if the sustainable carrying capacity of the world is 6, 9 or 2 billion people. But we do know that how heavily we tread on the earth has an impact on that number. We know that the rich world's addiction to shopping, driving, eating, spending on guns and indulging ourselves is doing more than its fair share to contribute to lowering the carrying capacity of the world. We know that the global community does not do nearly enough to redress the all too obvious injustices of the world. It is time to change.

Shahin Shafaei case study

'You are wrong,' says Shahin Shafaei, 'to focus on the economics of migration. The vast majority of people who leave their homes are not looking for a place to make more money, they are fleeing political persecution.' He should know.

On 19 June 2000, Shafaei and 111 other passengers on a leaky Indonesian fishing boat washed ashore on Ashmore Reef, a tiny dot in the Timor Sea some 500 miles west of Darwin. From there he was taken to the Curtin Detention Centre, a prison in an air force base in the middle of the desert in far-north Western Australia.

Shafaei is a playwright, director and actor. Working in his hometown of Tehran, in Iran, Shahin's first play out of university was banned after its first performance when the judges from the Ministry of Culture considered it too racy for their liking. He didn't have much luck after that either: of the eleven plays he wrote, only three received approval from the Ministry to move to rehearsal stage, and only one of those was permitted to run for any amount of time. The men from the Ministry lost patience with him once and for all in 1996. They banned him from writing any further plays.

A ban such as this is easier to send down than to impose, however, and Shafaei, dedicated to his craft, continued to write. Between his ban in 1996 and 2000, he started five or six different plays, but completed only one: he reckons his best work. For a playwright, though, writing is only one part of the equation. The complete experience is to see the play performed on stage. So when a friend studying for his PhD at Tehran University begged Shafaei to let him perform his work for his final examination, they convinced each other that nothing bad could come of it—it was a closed exam only for the examiners. But there were some radical, almost revolutionary bits in it, and these were the parts overheard by the university's security guards one Friday—Islam's holy day.

Shafaei is still thankful that he had not attended that particular rehearsal—the security guards raided the room and captured everybody present. Shafaei's friend, preparing for his PhD examination, has not been heard from since. Hearing of the raid, Shafaei knew that it was only a matter of time before the security guards found his name on the university's attendance register. He fled.

Malaysia is the only country that will allow people from Iran in without a visa. They receive two weeks entry on arrival at the airport. But Shafaei knew that diplomatic relations between Malaysia and Iran are so good that he could not stay in Malaysia for fear of deportation. He was approached by a people smuggler in the lobby of his Kuala Lumpur hotel: 'If you are of Middle Eastern appearance,' he says, 'they swarm all over you.'

An attempt to escape to Germany with a false passport was aborted at the airport after a fellow traveller was taken for questioning by the authorities. With only three days left on his two weeks' Malaysian visa, Shafaei was desperate for any solution. He was offered one: Australia.

Until then, Shafaei knew nothing of Australia, not even that it was an English-speaking country. But a desperate man will reach for any ray of hope, so he handed the smuggler US$2000 to get him as far as Indonesia, and promised him another US$2000 for the Indonesia–Australia leg. It bought him 30 days in a safe house outside of Jakarta, seven days and seven nights on a boat that was not seaworthy, and 21 months in a desert prison camp courtesy of the Howard Government.

At Curtin, Shafaei's proficient English made him the unofficial spokesman and lawyer for many of his fellow prisoners. From this he learned that it is wrong to think of refugees in economic terms: 'Most would fight hard to stay in their homeland, even under terrible economic stress, just because it is their home. But, like me, they cannot stay.'

Now a resident in Sydney on a three-year temporary protection visa, Shafaei has returned to his beloved stagecraft. At the beginning of 2003 he wrote a one-man stage play about his time in detention, which he has performed in front of some 6000 people in a tour that took him throughout the eastern states. After each performance he takes questions. Often people ask him what they can do to change the government's approach to refugee issues. He has three suggestions:

1   **Write to your MP.** Members of parliament take their corre-
     spondents seriously. Often MPs are elected with less then
     1000 votes. If each of the fifty people who come to a play were
     to write to them they would have to take it to parliament, or
     fear losing their jobs. If you want to go on writing, write to the
     minister responsible, and the prime minister, and ask them
     why they are doing what they are doing.

2   **Get in touch with people inside detention centres.** If rela-
     tionships between the refugee and local communities are
     strengthened, governments will have a harder time demonis-
     ing the people.

3   **Talk about these issues in your everyday life.** With your
     colleagues, friends, parents, children, students or teachers.
     You will find that many people are as concerned as you, but
     don't feel able to speak about serious issues with others. By
     discussing stuff, ideas come on to the table: the first step to
     really changing the world.

Does he miss home? 'Desperately,' says Shafaei.

Is he building a new life in Australia? He looks at his hands:
'I find it much easier not to think about the future, but to focus on
the everyday, to do what *I* believe is right, and to fight for my
beliefs—something I was doing in Iran, and enjoying.'

7
CORPORATE POWER

Some things we agree on. One of those things is that, like it or not, living an ordinary life in the twenty-first century means being part of something very, very big. Take the following two insignificant vignettes from our plainly ordinary lives.

A random Tuesday in September, 5 p.m. Mike is driving home from a meeting across Sydney, stops at a service station to fill up with petrol and buy a bottle of mineral water. Arriving home, five-year-old Max is in front of the television playing PlayStation and three-year-old Joel is in the backyard playing with his yellow truck. Claire is sitting at the table reading a textbook.

Over in London, the day is just starting. Breakfast for Adrian is toast, coffee and a Nutri-Grain bar in the car on the way to the train station. Meanwhile, little Ella has turned on Cartoon Network before school and Linda is scanning *The Times*.

Innocent enough routines, probably repeated in hundreds of millions, or even billions of minor variations across the globe every day. Without even stopping to think, almost every moment of every day, the intricate web of transactions that make up the complex of commerce, the tower of trade, the world of global business are subtly reinforced and strengthened . . . by us.

How so?

Toyota, which made Mike's car, had annual revenues of

$108 billion (all figures are from 2002 and in US dollars). This sits between, say, the GDP of Portugal ($105 billion) and the total tax take of the Commonwealth of Australia ($119 billion). The petrol was sold by BP, a minuscule fraction of its $180 billion total sales , which put it slightly above the GDP of Saudi Arabia, at $173 billion. Neverfail, the manufacturer of the mineral water casually purchased at the BP service station, is part of Coca-Cola Amatil, a $2 billion spin-off from Atlanta-based Coca-Cola Company (revenues of close to $5 billion).

Max, the PlayStation zombie, is an early capture for Sony, a company that raked in $57 billion in revenues, with over 161 000 people on the payroll. That's not quite as high as the GDP of Pakistan, but Pakistan contains more than 140 million people. Even little Joel's Tonka truck is produced by a global toy behemoth, Hasbro, which pulls in revenues of nearly $3 billion, and Claire's textbook is produced by Penguin, owned by a $7 billion-Brit corporation, Pearson.

Over in London the portrait is equally easy to paint—not even Adrian's toast is free from the taint of global capitalism. The bread, purchased from the local Tesco supermarket (revenues $48 billion), was baked by Hovis, part of Rank Hovis McDougall (private equity firm Doughty Hanson & Co. snapped them up in 2000 for close to $2 billion—it says it wants to grow the business into a pan-European food manufacturing concern and then sell it off some time in the future). The coffee is by Lavazza, an Italian company with group turnover close to $1 billion, just from coffee; Nutri-Grain bar by Kellogg's (revenues $8.3 billion); car by Ford (revenues $162 billion, equal to Hong Kong's GDP); rail trip to London by Connex (part of French giant Vivendi, revenues $68 billion), a company so lousy it was stripped of its franchise to run trains by the British government. Ella's entertainment is courtesy of American showbusiness octopus Time Warner, with revenues of $41 billion, while Linda's *Times* feeds Rupert Murdoch's $30 billion beast News International.

Big business, it seems, is everywhere. It sits at the breakfast table, drives with us to school, infiltrates our clothes and inhabits our homes and workplaces. It informs us and keeps us ignorant, it encourages our bad habits, and profits from their treatment. It is with us at our laying down and at our waking. Like Charlie Chaplin in *Modern Times* (filmed in the middle of the Depression), we are but cogs in the wheels of the great machinery of the global corporation. Stamped 'customer' at birth, the brand remains till we die. And, short of stranding ourselves on a desert island, it seems there is little we can do about it.

This, Mike and Adrian can agree on. But we don't agree about what this means for how we should live our lives in Crunch Time.

Corporate power—a lesson from history

Here's what Adrian reckons. The fact that enormous global corporations dominate our lives is neither novel, nor especially scary. Today's big business is altogether less powerful and less threatening than it has been for hundreds of years. To prove the point, take a look at this modern landmark of the City of London, one of the world's great financial centres—One Lime Street.

Today it is a complex and twisted mountain of inverted stainless steel pipes and fittings, an award-winning architectural marvel built by Richard Rogers (Lord Rogers of Riverside), into which each day hundreds of insurance brokers disappear, toting their leather folders and obscure papers. Here, the risks of global capitalism are underwritten by the syndicates that call this building, and the insurance market that sits within it—Lloyd's of London—home.

Impressive as it is, the kind of twenty-first century business that flows through One Lime Street today pales into insignificance compared to the enterprises that were planned and executed on this spot just a hundred and fifty years ago. Then, the site was headquarters to the most significant global corporation the world has ever seen, or is ever likely to see, and the directors behind their leather writing desks exercised the kind of power that would make the chiefs of BP, Toyota, News International and the rest green with envy.

At the height of its reign, the *United Company of Merchants of England Trading to the East Indies*—better known as the East India Company—had an army of 200 000 and really did rule the world. Its authority extended across what we know today as India, Pakistan, Bangladesh, Burma, Singapore and Hong Kong. A fifth of the world's population was under its power. At various stages in its 274-year history, under the auspices of trade, it militarily defeated Imperial China, occupied the Philippines and conquered Java.

The company was granted a Royal Charter—an enforceable monopoly—from Queen Elizabeth I on 31 December 1600. Initially a speculative venture to trade pepper and spices from Indonesia, it became rich by conquering India and laying down the foundations of the British Empire.

Three decades before Australia's First Fleet set sail, and two decades before disgruntled American colonists threw East India Company tea chests into Boston Harbor, the company's most brilliant servant, Robert Clive, engineered a local coup in Bengal. He wrote it up as the Battle of Plassey, after a somewhat dubious victory, and ended up running the place. Administering an entire country required armed forces and armed forces required taxes. Whalloping the Indians militarily, the East India

---

Trade cannot be maintained without war or war without trade.

Jan Pieterzoon Coen, 1614
on how to do business in India

Company won itself the right to tax over 20 million people, revenues of some two to three million pounds a year—the riches of an entire continent. Much of this was shipped back to London to the pleasure of the company's directors. A dozen or so years after the company took over running Bengal, there were scores of rich Englishmen and—owing to an 'unfortunate' famine shortly after—millions of dead Bengalis.

The history of the Honourable Company includes swash-buckling stories that would make the hair on the back of the necks of the most swaggering Crunch Time corporate executives stand up. These were the corporate gunslingers who hired Captain Kidd to undertake pirate raids in the South Seas, attacking any ships that sailed under the flag of Britain's enemies. These were the wheeler-dealers who leased St Helena to the British government as an upmarket Guantanamo Bay for Napoleon to see out his final days. These were the repressive rulers who provoked the Indian uprising of 1857. This was the era before 'corporate social responsibility', and the company's executives pioneered the kinds of business practices that get modern multinationals pilloried and their managements (occasionally) jailed.

Today's fat cats, insider traders and dodgy dealers are nothing in comparison. The East India Company enriched its corporate elite to a degree barely comprehensible by today's standards. After the 32-year-old Robert Clive installed a compliant local to help him run Bengal, the entire contents of its treasury were 'offered' to him, making him unfathomably rich. At a public inquiry into the probity of the affair, Clive's defence was simple: he could have had the lot, but only took most of it. More than the massive salaries and dubious methods, the company pioneered multinational exploitation of the global 'South' (as the poor world has become known, much to the chagrin of Australians and New Zealanders).

Back in the eighteenth century, when the East India Company was at its height, fashionable Europe craved cottons, silk, spices, porcelain and a decadent new drink: tea. These came from India and China, but the Indians and Chinese didn't crave European woolly undergarments and other such western manufactured delights. So the easterners made a lot of money—gold, and especially silver, flowed from west to east.

The East India Company forcibly stopped this transfer of bullion when it started helping itself to chunks of India, and began using the southern continent's own wealth to pay for the exports of its goods back to Britain. Many Indians believe that the East India Company's way of doing business was the earliest cause of their country's ongoing poverty. When the company arrived in southern Asia, India was a rich nation with sophisticated industries of its own. Britain plundered it, and used the money it found there to fuel its own industrial expansion. A little later on, the company used Indian-grown opium to make millions out of importing addiction to China.

When the company's charter finally expired in 1874, *The London Times* noted, 'it accomplished a work such as in the whole history of the human race no other company ever attempted and as such is ever likely to attempt in the years to come'.

Rupert Murdoch, eat your heart out.

Corporate power—a lesson from today

We don't necessarily live in the age of the most heinous corporate excesses, but still, as we saw at the beginning of this chapter, there is no doubt that we live in an age of corporate behemoths. While the East India Company was indeed the daddy of all global corporate monoliths, it did rule at a time when there weren't that many other corporations spanning the globe and bending its resources to their own ends. Today, there are over a thousand companies with revenues in excess of a billion American dollars.

Mike picked up the story in a phone call that random Tuesday evening in September. 'It's not about cinnamon and chintz any more. It's not even about planting flags in far-off parts of the world any more. It's much more insidious than that.'

Mike feels that in Crunch Time, corporations are complicit in perhaps the greatest conspiracy ever: the perpetuation of western, consumerist values across the globe, the systematic plundering of the earth's resources for toys and trinkets, designer baby clothes, mobile phone handsets, consumer electronics, lifestyle excess, luxury travel . . . the list goes on. Corporations, their marketeers and advertisers, take advantage of our everyday human desires and insecurities to sell us a bunch of stuff we don't need, to perpetuate a wasteful system that—as we have seen in earlier chapters—the rest of the world simply cannot ever afford.

From Mike's bookshelf, here are just three of the books whose hundreds of pages outline the charges against the twenty-first century multinationals:

- *No Logo:* Canadian journalist Naomi Klein's account of the not-so-slow progress of corporate branding into every part of modern life: our cities and landscapes, our youth, our education systems; the way brands are used to prise big profits out of customers whether they can afford it or not; and the anti-corporate movement's protests and boycotts against all this.
- *The Silent Takeover:* UK academic Noreena Hertz argues that the declining power of the state and the increasing power of business over the past 30 years is undermining democracy and leaving us at the mercy of the market.
- *One Market Under God:* Social critic Thomas Frank claims that western society has elevated the market and its non-values above everything else.

Want more? Type in 'anti-corporate' on Amazon.com and over 40 titles come up with catchy names such as *Corporation Nation*,

Earth for Sale and the not-so-catchy *Insurrection: Citizen Challenges to Corporate Power*.

'Naomi Klein?' replied Adrian. 'What better example of a global brand is there than Naomi Klein? I'm surprised she hasn't started putting "no logo" on an exclusive line of clothes distributed through Wal-Mart.'

It's true, the success of the anti-corporate argument has relied on exactly the technology and tools the corporate world uses to achieve its own objectives. Cynicism aside though, Mike insisted that the abuse of corporate power wasn't consigned to history. The crimes levelled at the institution of the corporation are many. Apart from the 'conspiracy to promote consumerism' charge, which we'll look at later, here are the big ones.

1 Exploitation—the sweatshop issue

You're the production manager of a US-based children's clothing company and have been asked to recommend where to locate a new factory. You have been told to base your decision on cost and productivity. How about the home of the free?

Well, in the US there's no national minimum wage, but factory workers make around US$7 an hour. Australia's minimum wage makes Aussies a little dearer to hire at US$7.90. Brits have a minimum wage too, they come in at around US$7.50. The Germans don't have a minimum wage but they're highly unionised with big government-mandated social costs passed on to employers. So should the factory stay in Idaho?

Take a look at the wages in 'developing' countries in the box on page 178. Indonesia looks a little more attractive than Idaho, even with the security situation. Why not subcontract your manufacturing to a developing nation where workers will spend their lives producing your goods at a fraction of the cost of the folks back home, and without demanding any of the pesky limitations on hours worked, let alone demands for pensions, holidays and sick pay, or health and safety provisions?

Country	Factory workers' hourly pay (US$)
Guatemala	0.67
El Salvador	0.60
Mexico	0.50
Honduras	0.43
Haiti	0.30
China	0.28
Nicaragua	0.23
Indonesia	0.20
Bangladesh	0.17–0.37
Romania	0.13–0.20
Russia	0.11–0.56
Burma	0.04

Source: *Take it Personally*.

In fact while you're at it, why don't you close down your existing factories and move them to more cost effective locations too?

Making things (T-shirts or software) where the cost of labour is lower certainly makes sense for management (but not the newly unemployed staff in our old factories). It means cheaper goods, higher profits (higher bonuses!) and it means people who would be otherwise poor and unemployed in developing countries now have jobs. And let's face it, corporations didn't make countries poor (well, maybe they did a couple of centuries ago, but that was then and this is now).

The problem with this scenario, however, is with the regulation (or lack of) of jobs in developing countries. Workers and employers aren't paying for the kind of welfare and healthcare provision western countries demand. Conditions aren't regulated, regulations aren't enforced, and enforcement isn't acted upon. Stories of fourteen-hour shifts, seven-day working weeks, child labour, bonded labour and the worst kind of Victorian workhouse conditions are not difficult to unearth.

And the problems don't end there.

By electing to pay low wages—either directly or at arm's length through subcontracting—and operating in countries where standards are lower, companies are complicit in the not-so-slow transfer of wealth from the poor world to the rich that we have seen in earlier chapters. While sweatshop workers put in the hours, the rat race's big winners in New York and London and the rest of the rich world, and that includes us, make off with the cheese.

This is what many of the world's best-known brands have been caught doing: producing clothes and other goods at a tiny cost in some crummy third world hellhole factory, and then packaging, advertising and retailing them at designer prices in elegantly furnished stores. It's a very Crunch Time kind of crime. But it is joined in the dock by a much older sort of crime, and one that is not going away.

2 Corruption

We've already seen in the 'Democracy' chapter that the corporate sector dominates national debates through the obscene amounts of money it provides to political parties and lobbyists. Corrupt, clearly. But, corporate corruption comes in all shapes and sizes. Here's a little example from the capital of capitalism, Manhattan.

Jack Grubman, a $20m-a-year telecoms' analyst with Citigroup, decides he must get his two little daughters into a plush Upper East Side nursery. He approaches Sandy Weill, CEO of the world's largest bank, Citigroup, the acknowledged king of Wall Street, and asks if he might be able to swing it for the Grubman twins to get into the 92nd Street Y. The boss is happy to help. Calls are made. Citigroup pledges US$1 million to the nursery school. Places are found. Does Sandy want anything for keeping one of his top analysts sweet? Well, Sandy is a director of AT&T, and kind-hearted Jack apparently agrees to recommend that his investors buy AT&T stock. The favour is returned, the only victims—the suckers who bought duff stock on the analyst's say-so (and perhaps the parents whose child-care places have suddenly evaporated).

Corruption also goes beyond the snobbish concerns of Wall Street's superstars. Take French oil company, Elf. At the time of writing, a massive trial was underway during which the ex-president of Elf, Loik Le Floch-Prigent, confirmed an open secret: for decades the state-owned energy giant provided cover for all manner of political shenanigans, including overt bribery and secret political party funding. General De Gaulle as president of the country created the 'black box' system that enabled Elf to grease its way into oil contracts and challenge its British and American rivals away from the gaze of French tax inspectors. But guess what? Putting a slush fund intended for bribery at the disposal of executives corrupt enough to engage in such practices was like passing round a vodka bottle at an AA meeting. The weak and greedy (who in this case happened also to be the rich and powerful) just helped themselves.

After eight years of investigating, the trial opened in March 2003 with 37 defendants and 80 lawyers crowded into a Paris courtroom. Revelations were rife. In the space of four years, between 1989 and 1993, the year before Elf was privatised, senior Elf executives are alleged to have skimmed more than half a billion dollars from Elf's 'black box' of secret funds straight into their personal accounts, often with the approval of then president of France, François Mitterrand. Le Floch-Prigent is accused, among other things, of using Elf money to buy an A$14.5 million flat in Paris, a chateau near the capital and to pay off his ex-wife, Fatima Belaid—also in the dock—in an A$5 million divorce settlement. During Le Floch-Prigent's tenure, the amount of money sloshing through the secret accounts, known as 'the kitchen', multiplied tenfold, with A$8.5 million a year allotted just for paying off French politicians—names mentioned include the current president's.

Everywhere they operate, corporate types have an understandable tendency to seek political favours, allied with the cash to buy them. They bend and break the rules, they push the boundaries, and they do it for the personal gain of the

---

Ye Olde corporate corruption

Corporate corruption and misbehaviour comes in all sorts of forms, and has done so for centuries. Writing in the eighteenth century British journalist Dr Joseph Manning revealed in *The Nature of Bread, Honestly and Dishonestly Made* that unscrupulous millers and bakers were adding alum, lead and the ash from burnt animal bones to flour to make their bread look whiter. The same year the book came out parliament passed laws against adulterating flour. They were mostly ignored.

---

powerful people in the company. It is occasionally blatant, always repugnant.

3 Unaccountability

By dint of their size, power and wealth, global corporates are arguably the single most important influence on the global economy today. But corporations aren't accountable to the people over whose lives they hold sway. They might produce accounts, but as the bosses of Enron noted, getting them endorsed merely requires the right kind of accountant . . . not too difficult to find, apparently.

We don't vote for the management of corporations. The rules they follow, where there are any, are determined in shady meetings in five-star hotels, under the auspices of bodies that are above the states we live in: the World Trade Organization, or the Council of Foreign Relations, or the Trilateral Commission (a body of over 300 senior people which meets every three years to thrash out the rules of globalisation), or the World Bank. The rules that these bodies (unanswerable to anyone) decide upon are the rules by which the game is played—like it or not.

Businessmen rail against any restrictions. The chairman of Dow Chemical once dreamed publicly 'of buying an island owned by no nation and of establishing the world headquarters of the Dow company on the truly neutral ground of such an island, beholden to no nation or society'. Multinationals threaten to up-sticks and go elsewhere whenever governments have the temerity to threaten to raise taxes or toughen safety standards.

Corporations are supposed to be accountable to the law, to government and to their shareholders. But they spend money on lobbying to weaken or change laws, they spend money on politicians (see Elf) and, if they keep paying dividends, their shareholders aren't likely to ask too many questions either. The 'government relations' and lobbying power of corporations is not matched by anything on the other side of the political debate, so inevitably big business gets a better hearing than little you—or me. By this argument, those who are the victims of pro-business policies and decisions, including sweatshop workers, local farmers and businessmen who are bankrupted, and the global 'South', are ground underfoot by the remorseless march of heartless global capitalism.

So there you have Mike's shortlist of allegations against the corporate world—exploitation, corruption and unaccountability. But by the end of the phone call he'd thrown in the rest. The world is becoming blander, a Starbucks and McDonald's on every corner. Our ecosystems are being destroyed as global corporations reach into the furthest corners of the earth and rape the ground, sea and air, only to return home to count the profits. The anti-logic of corporate operations has turned the world into a 'race-to-the-bottom' as countries and regions within them compete to provide the lowest standards and most attractive environment for the profiteers. They don't pay tax. They're amoral, dirty, dehumanising, aggressive and generally B-A-D.

The case for the defence

It's never good to interrupt someone in full flow. Adrian decided not to point out that it's a bit rich to sit in centrally heated or air conditioned comfort, travel slowly but comfortably in privately owned cars (fuel courtesy of the heinous and blood-thirsty oil industry), entertain kids with the poison fruit of Sony and Time Warner and, when the contradictions end up giving us a headache, pop a GlaxoSmithKline pill to make us feel a bit better, then bitch about the terrible influence of global corporations. Look around. Everything we have and every-thing we do is pretty much owed to the corporation. Without the innovation of the joint stock company and its ability to risk large amounts of capital on audacious projects we would still be living in the dark ages.

'Mike,' Adrian eventually said, 'you're way off track.'

Companies have their faults, for sure. Bosses, being people, often get weird ideas about their place in the world and go off the rails. But when they do, they get caught. That then simply prompts society to figure out tougher ways to police executives who've diverged too far from what most of us think is accept-able business practice. The then US Treasury Secretary Paul O'Neill memorably described Enron's $100 billion failure as a 'triumph of American capitalism'. Whether the shareholders and workers whose wealth went down the plughole agree is a different matter; what he was *trying* to say was that it all comes out in the wash in the end.

What about the argument that the power of corporations is growing? The most frequently cited statistics show how companies are now bigger than most countries. Sarah Anderson and John Cavanagh of America's Institute for Policy Studies, in a report called *Top 200: The Rise of Corporate Power*, said:

> Of the 100 largest economies in the world, 51 are corporations; only 49 are countries (based on a comparison of corporate sales

> and country GDPs). To put this in perspective, General Motors
> is now bigger than Denmark; DaimlerChrysler is bigger than
> Poland; Royal Dutch/Shell is bigger than Venezuela; IBM is bigger
> than Singapore; and Sony is bigger than Pakistan.

Scary stuff. We played around with some of those comparisons at the start of this chapter. Scary, yes, but totally wrong. Comparing a corporation's revenues with a country's gross domestic product (GDP) looks good on paper but, honestly, it's apples and oranges. A country's GDP—with all its faults as a yardstick of progress and wellbeing—is actually a measure of the total value added of all the products, materials, goods and services produced by that country over the course of the year— in other words, profit. A company's revenues are just the amount of cash that rolled in the door that year, the vast bulk of which has to be spent on paying for the cost of producing the goods and services sold, taxes, employee benefits and all sorts of stuff. So the real size of Toyota by the equivalent of GDP is actually its net profits, closer to $4 billion than the $128 billion figure we quoted earlier. That makes it nowhere near the size of Portugal's economy. Instead it's about half the size of an economic basketcase like Zimbabwe. But it did produced 6 million cars in 2003, giving jobs to 66 000 people.

There are big differences too between the powers of countries and those of companies. The world's biggest corporation in terms of revenue, Wal-Mart, made profits of just over $8 billion, close to the GDP of Cameroon. Cameroon has 14.7 million citizens, Wal-Mart has 1.2 million employees. But the state of Cameroon can do a bunch of stuff that Wal-Mart cannot. It can raise an army and a police force, raise taxes, enforce systems and ways of life, and hold political sway over all its people. It can even produce Africa's best soccer team. Wal-Mart, on the other hand, just sells stuff, and distributes its profits to those who hold its shares. Cameroon's land, people and resources will likely be there long after Wal-Mart is consigned to corporate history.

If an employee, customer or shareholder of Wal-Mart gets cheesed off with the company, they can just go elsewhere— buy their clothes at K-Mart, for instance, quit their job or sell their shares. A citizen of Cameroon is a subject of that country, for better or for worse. Emigration is a radical solution for disgruntlement. And corporations, even the biggest and best, do get binned on a regular basis.

Tom Peters, the wacky management guru who brought us the 'the brand called you' in the 'Money and work' chapter, wrote a book called *In Search of Excellence* in 1982 in which he looked at the characteristics of 48 'excellent' companies. Excellent or not, the 'ex' part was right. Two thirds of them are now ex-companies. Yesterday's Wal-Mart, anti-globalisation whipping-boy McDonald's, has had to shut down its operations in three countries and is closing nearly 200 branches. Either French cheese-makers storming their restaurants has scared them into global retreat, or consumers are just fed up with eating their burgers. Goodbye global domination, hello commercial reality. And the globalisation of trade and investment means corporations are facing tougher competition from each other too. There are more companies operating in almost every line of business.

'Okay,' replies Mike, 'let's take our three accusations one at a time and see how your arguments fare against them.'

1 Exploitation

Nobody would say it is a good thing for workers to be employed in horrible conditions below a living wage. But the fact that companies operate around the world, sell their goods back in the west and have a shareholder base in the west means that they have to have an eye on standards wherever they operate. Shareholders and consumers do care, so the companies have to care. Part of this is due to Naomi Klein and the rest of the anti-corporate crowd who raise awareness. Look at Nike—pilloried for contracting work to sweatshops. It took the criticism seriously and now imposes a serious code of conduct on its suppliers. The sweatshop problem is solvable in the case of big multinationals. Studies have shown that multinational firms pay more for labour where they operate because they have to have an eye on standards, and because they are more efficient.

The sweatshop problem is far more of an issue for smaller, private companies that produce goods that aren't readily identifiable as branded. Look at that little plastic figure on your key chain or the made-in-China toys that are so cheap down at the supermarket, or those unbranded clothes for sale in the pile-'em-high sell-'em-cheap supermarket down the road. How do you know the conditions under which they are made? You just don't, because they don't come from a reputable company, or have a reputable brand. What you do know is that companies that do sell branded goods are held to account for the standard and values of those brands.

In any case, without international investment, most of these jobs would never exist. The challenge, then, is to make sure they are decent jobs—and Klein and her crowd are doing a good job of piling on the pressure to make sure this happens. As poor countries get richer because of the investment that these companies are making, standards there will rise as they have all over the developed world.

2 Corruption

Crime is crime. Corporate criminals who rip off shareholders or pension funds are no better, and often much worse, than simple bank robbers. Chuck 'em in the clink. If that is not happening, strengthen your laws and sort out your politicians—they are in charge of controlling crime.

When bad stuff happens, such as Enron and the rest, rules get strengthened. Accounting standards and corporate governance is much stronger now than it was before all these disasters. Whether it is strong enough remains to be seen, but new laws and executive criminals in handcuffs show that the system works, more or less. In developed countries, the regulatory demands on companies are clearly increasing—as they should be—in areas like accounting standards.

More difficult to deal with are the insidious links between politicians and big business—of the Elf kind. Once again, what matters is the robustness of the legal system, and also the corporate culture in which these crimes happen. Culture is down to the people within the companies, which is down to the individuals like you and me who work for them.

3 Accountability

Okay, we don't directly vote for company management, but we do vote with our cash. As we saw in the 'Money and work' chapter, the owners of these big corporations are you and I through our pension funds and investments. Sure, individually we don't have much clout, but together we do. Why do you think companies get so scared when it looks like their reputations are going down the gurgler? Look at Shell, for instance.

Greenpeace gave Shell a hugely hard time when it was going to dump the Brent Spar oil platform into the North Sea. Consumers across Europe boycotted Shell products. The company lost something like 20 per cent of its market share in Germany in the month the story was in the news. In the end the company backed down. It turned the platform around and towed it to a fjord in Norway where it was expensively dismantled.

All of this is possible only because we live in societies where the activities of companies like this are open to scrutiny. Companies have to publish tons of information on what they are up to—and so they should. But the amount of information they publish is only getting bigger. More and more are publishing environmental and social reports as well as financial stuff. Even if you think it's total greenwash, it is still more than any companies in non-democratic, non-market-led societies do.

What do we know about China's top companies? Even if you're interested and speak Chinese, the information just isn't there. Don Tapscott, a Canadian management guru, believes the future for corporations is 'nakedness'—being open and transparent, revealing everything they do all the time, on the web, in the press, to whoever wants to know. Companies that don't do this will suffer.

'No,' says Adrian, 'corporations are just an easy target. They're big. Like all of us they can do bad stuff. And they undoubtedly command vast swathes of resources. But it is difficult to point the finger at the institution of the corporation per se.'

So here we come to a bit of an impasse.

We agree our lives are dominated by the products of big business. We can even agree that those products are often a good thing—Mike likes that his safe and reliable car transports him home from business meetings, that Joel has a nicely produced big yellow truck to play with, and that Penguin's ability to publish high quality textbooks cheaply allows Claire to study at home rather than spend her time at the library or not study at all. Adrian enjoys his toast and coffee and the rest of the accoutrements of a modern lifestyle, many of which were not enjoyed by our ancestors who did not live in an age of corporate titans. But we diverge when it comes to thinking about how to curb some of the excesses that inevitably occur when one sector of society comes to command so many of its resources.

For Mike and his Kleinist anti-corporateers, the answer can only be in a radical change in lifestyle—a mass turning away from the fruits of corporate production to a different, more sustainable lifestyle of the kind we described in the 'Environment' chapter. How might this happen? Through protest, through the kind of movements seen in Seattle and Genoa at the World Trade meetings and other anti-globalism riots. Through awareness-raising, distribution of information over the Internet through sites such as sweatshop.org or Global

Exchange. Through a steady and determined effort to change both the way we live and the way companies are allowed to interact with society.

For Adrian, the answer is not so much the magical 'dawning of consciousness' that is hoped for by the new international left. Corporations have power, no doubt, and they use it to their own ends. But surely this, then, is the secret: align corporations' interests more closely with those of society in general. The ballyhoo protest of Klein and her chums has helped enormously in this. Corporations with global brands are now terrified of being caught out doing the wrong thing, and so they should be. If the system has faults, which it does now and will into the future, then surely our efforts should be bent towards plugging those faults, rather than pulling down the whole edifice and all the good things that go with it. Fundamentally, we do like our lives. If it ain't totally broke, why try and totally fix it?

There are good, established ways to work to change the system, to limit power where it needs to be limited, and to act to influence things to change. We have examined lots of them in this book. In the end, the answer has to be something in the middle. Mike is not about to take his family off to a desert island . . . he has a hard enough time getting Max to turn off the PlayStation when it's time to go to school, or avoiding big brand mineral water at the service station. But that doesn't necessarily make him a bad person. We are all limited by our time and place, and there is a constant tension between what we want to achieve in our lives, our hopes and dreams, and the demands placed on us by the broader concerns for the state of society and the future we are building for our children and their generation.

Blowing the whistle case study

There are times in life, however, when things move beyond the theoretical and the stark reality of corporate power and wrongdoing is staring you straight in the face. Once a senior buyer for one of Australia's top retail chains, Jay Berger discovered that things don't always go your way when you try to work with the system to resolve real issues. In early 2000, the company moved Berger into a new job as an 'indent rebuyer' of general merchandise—somebody who buys the bits and pieces—suitcases, plates and cups, transistor radios and the like—from overseas. As the new girl on the job, Berger asked a lot of questions. Often they were questions which her supervisor wasn't too comfortable answering. With fifteen years in the wholesale fruit and vegetable business—according to Berger a snake pit of corrupt practices, kickbacks and rorting—she reckons she knows a scam when she sees one. At her new company she found a suspicious lack of documentation for a raft of purchases, containers full of, say, food trays would just arrive, with no accompanying paperwork. 'I could see suitcases coming in, and going out, but there were no scanned sales from the stores coming through,' she says.

What really worried Berger was when she went to check the situation with her supervisor, he would pull out a purchase order book from his desk and write it out—in her name. During her time in the department, she discovered some 700 containers of stuff just sitting in customs' agents warehouses, with goods regularly disappearing from them, indefensible supply practices and, she says, quite blatant rorting on behalf of the senior buying executives. 'I know that corruption goes on in buying,' she says, 'that is why a lot of people go into it in the first place. Kickbacks are easy to get and most people just turn their heads in the other direction.'

For Berger, though, things came to a head over one particular container for which the paperwork was clearly missing. 'I just kept asking questions. In the end I was told to mind my own business. Problem was, it was my business, because my name was on the purchase order.'

In the end, Berger confided in a senior colleague in a different part of the organisation who put a call in to internal audit. Late-night meetings at head office were arranged, and documents were exchanged. External auditors were brought into the department to investigate. Although nobody knew that it was Berger who had invited the probe, some of her colleagues guessed. 'They all started treating me like a piece of crap,' she says.

The issue came to a head one day in the middle of the investigation when Berger went into the office to find her superiors throwing all the purchase ledgers and other documents, into the wheelie bins. In tears, Berger fled to the car park and phoned the chief executive of the company, threatening to go outside the organisation to the media unless something serious was done. The chief of internal audit rang her back.

'Don't worry about it,' he said, 'it's just more rope for them to hang themselves.'

'I began to wonder how high this went,' says Berger.

In the end, Berger was moved to a succession of other jobs within the company and then, after no suitable position for her could be found, she left. Applying for other jobs within the industry, Berger suddenly found she was unemployable.

For Berger, whistleblowing is not something you choose, you either have to do it or you don't. Many people turn away when they see corporate corruption, wanting just an easy life. Here are her tips for those with more backbone:

1 Get help

There are support groups that understand the pressures whistle-blowers are under, and can provide emotional and legal support. 'You have to be extremely careful about *how* you go about blowing the whistle if you want to get through it with your sanity intact,' she says. 'You will not have a normal life after. You *must* think about that before you decide to do it.'

Cynthia Kardell, who works with Whistleblowers Australia, says that you need to get your ducks in a row before you make your move. 'Get all your resignation and legal issues out of the way. Understand that your life is going to change and prepare yourself for it emotionally.'

2 Know your enemy

You can expect the company to come at you with everything it's got, legally and personally. Substantiate and document your position and ensure you have covered yourself from every angle. Understand the company's weak spots, for example, an aversion to negative media coverage or its relationships with its customers and suppliers, and be prepared to use those weak spots against it. 'They will be merciless with you, so be prepared to be the same,' says Berger.

Kardell adds, 'Many people think that others are just like them, and have difficulty coming to terms with evil when it confronts them. We in the west like to think that we are more civilised than others, but when it comes down to it, good and bad exists everywhere.'

3 Don't get too emotionally involved

It might be that you have spent five days a week, 48 weeks of the year at it for the last umpteen years, but in the end it is only a job and the company is only a company, not a proxy for your own soul. Getting overly emotional about the issue will only aid your enemy's cause by blunting your own effectiveness as an agent of change.

Kardell says, 'People naively can't believe that others can behave so terribly badly, even when confronted by the evidence in front of their own eyes. They spend a lot of time wondering "but why, but why", not wanting to believe what's in front of their faces.'

8
GLOBALISATION

A few decades ago, it was still possible to leave home and go somewhere else: the architecture was different, the landscape was different, the language, lifestyle, dress, and values were different. That was a time when we could speak of cultural diversity. But with economic globalization, diversity is fast disappearing. The goal of the global economy is that all countries should be homogenized. When global hotel chains advertise to tourists that all their rooms in every city of the world are identical, they don't mention that the cities are becoming identical too: cars, noise, smog, corporate high-rises, violence, fast food, McDonalds, Nikes, Levis, Barbie Dolls, American TV and film. What's the point of leaving home?

This is from a two-page advertisement placed in the *New York Times* just before the Seattle meeting of the World Trade Organization that attracted the first and biggest anti-globalisation protests.

'Globalisation trashed for destroying the quality of the tourism experience', Adrian wrote to Mike about the ad.

We figured there were two ways of looking at this. And the rest . . . but let's start with two.

The first view says that the reason the apartment blocks in Bombay and Brisbane are identical is because, when presented with a choice between a village hut, a shanty town or a ghastly concrete apartment block, people will generally choose the apartment block—even if they come to regret it later. When presented with a shiny McDonald's burger or rice and manioc again, it will be McDonald's. Most people reckon they'd rather drive on an ugly spaghetti junction than not drive. These are all just the direct results of man's drive to achieve 'better' things. More than that, it is hypocritical and downright immoral for you, rich person, to enjoy the fruits of our progress—longer, healthier, better educated, more independent and richer lives— and to deny them to the rest of the world, just because you want to have somewhere interesting to go on your holiday.

The second perspective is different. This perspective says that people aren't free to make choices, and what choices they are presented with are determined by forces beyond their control. The choice isn't simply McDonald's versus rice and manioc, it's one type of society versus another. Often choices are made while staring down the barrel of a rifle—a real one or a metaphorical one.

The answer of course is that both of these hold true. Where globalisation is concerned the key to managing our way out of the Crunch Time bottleneck will be to balance these two perspectives, and it's not too much to say that it will be one of the greatest challenges human civilisation will have to face as we head further into the twenty-first century. To illustrate the first perspective we go to Japan, the second, Mauritania.

The land of the rising bun

McDonald's is far and away the number one target for anti-globalisation's ire. It marches across the globe carnivorously, swallowing cultures whole, laying the forests of the Amazon waste to feed the methane producing cows it needs for its burgers, destroying landscapes with its hated golden arches and taking the profits back to America, right? But McDonald's' first foray outside the shores of the United States was by invitation. In 1971, Den Fujita, a maverick law student out of Tokyo University, took himself to golden arches headquarters in Oak Brook, Illinois, and asked for the right to franchise McDonald's in Japan. Fujita took the brand and localised it—sort of . . . ever had a McTeriyaki burger? Delicious.

Fujita was the first person to single-handedly convert an entire culture to a new way of eating. From one store in Tokyo's Ginza district, Fujita's business opened some 3800 franchises, in the process making him the 27th richest man in the country in 2000 according to Japan's tax authorities. When the company floated on the stock exchange in 2001, its prospectus boasted that 10 000 stores will be opened by 2010. All of this was not because of a vindictive orange-haired clown on a crazed power trip, but because of the energy and ambition of Den Fujita and a Japanese society hankering for standardised hamburgers.

The flipside of this type of globalisation is the countless sushi restaurants, or Thai restaurants, or curry houses, or Chinese take-aways across Australia. People don't complain about globalisation when it enables two-way cultural flows. The problem is when it doesn't. And it often doesn't.

Make that a quarter pounder with camel cheese

Mauritania doesn't get too much of globalisation's spoils. This poor country is basically the Sahara with added sand, dunes and rock. Some of its poorest people—many living under the World Bank's absolute poverty line of $1 a day—still live the kind of nomadic existence that seems to reach back beyond the Bible stories into the prehistoric ages of humanity. Nomadism has a romantic appeal that evokes camel trains, blanket bags, lavishly appointed tents and the kinds of stores that sell ethnic rugs and scented candles. And it is romantic, if you're in love with camels.

Mauritania's nomads are camel herders. They live on them and off them. Camel hair is woven into cloth for making clothes, tents and rugs. The dung is burnt for fuel. The hides are cured into a tough leather for water pouches and shoes. And camel-steaks are a staple of the diet of West Africans. But, according to Nancy Abeiderrahmane, the owner of Mauritania's first camel dairy, the best thing about a camel is the milk. She says it is naturally low in fat and low in cholesterol, has as much protein as cow's milk and is less allergic. It has a high mineral content and a lot of vitamin C, and it is easy to digest because it doesn't curdle. It has half the fat of cow's milk and less sugar, and is good for diabetics because one of the proteins in it is similar to human insulin.

For the nomads of Mauritania, camel's milk is truly a boon. The reality of nomadism is that when what passes for camel pasture fails, they have been forced to resort to raiding and slave trading to make ends meet. And if that isn't possible they starve to death in what James Cameron, a famous British journalist, once called, 'One of those quiet, unreported famines hidden in the statistics, and still of little interest to the news pages and channels of our globalised media'. Like Den Fujita, Abeiderrahmane, arriving in Mauritania in 1970, came to see camel's milk as a marvellous opportunity for the Mauritanians. While Fujita was bringing burgers into the land of sushi, Abeiderrahmane wanted to export her camel's milk products, to bring back hard currency for the nomadic tribes.

She took her life savings and built Africa's first camel dairy to pasteurise and market the stuff. The company, called Tiviski after the local name for the Mauritanian spring, started up in the late 1980s with packaged camel milk, and then branched out into yoghurt and *crème fraiche*. Every day, trucks fan out from three collecting centres in towns along the Senegal River to pick up the white stuff, milked by hand by the nomads scattered around the region. Problem was that, because camel's milk doesn't curdle it doesn't convert easily to cheese, so any excess milk can't be stored and therefore it goes to waste.

Abeiderrahmane's challenge was how to stop the waste? She attracted the interest and funding of a wealthy western bureaucracy, the Food and Agriculture Organization, and went to see the people who know about cheese—the French. Hooking up with a professor from the wonderfully titled *Ecole Nationale Supérieure d'Agronomie et des Industries Alimentaires*, they developed a way to curdle the milk and make it into cheese, even in Mauritania's brutal climate. The cheese itself has the texture of brie but the taste of goat's cheese, and Abeiderrahmane, a good businesswoman, gave the product a romantic nomadic name—Caravane—and packaging, hopped on a plane and went to Europe with it.

Smart stores there loved the stuff. Abeiderrahmane came away with orders from the likes of Harrods in London and Fauchon in Paris.

Hold the cheese . . .

So here was a business proposition aimed at regularising the lives of some of the world's poorest people and developing a trade that could lift them out of the most abject poverty. A British woman had provided the seed capital and ideas, a French professor the technology, an NGO the development funding. A model development project. What could go wrong?

Problem: the free traders in Brussels had a thing or two to say about it. The first hurdle was that there was no classification for it. Camel's cheese wasn't a dairy product because EU law says that 'dairy products' only come from cows, buffalos, sheep or goats. Even when this was changed, bureaucrats in some countries decided they would slap serious tariffs on the product—despite the fact that there are no indigenous European camel-cheese makers to be threatened. Tiviski was told that they could appeal the decision but that would take time, and serious money. Even if the company won on tariffs, because the camels are not mechanically milked their cheese does not meet EU veterinary standards (designed to keep out

foot and mouth disease, of which camels are not known carriers)
so it couldn't bring camel cheese to Europe in any case.

Abeiderrahmane began looking at other, more distant,
markets—the US and Japan. Again camel's cheese was wel-
comed in delis and up-scale food stores. But there are no flights
there from Mauritania's Nouakchott Airport. Air Mauritanie
flies to only one potential market—Paris. And if the cheese
transits Paris, whatever its final destination, it is subject to EU
regulations anyhow. So the Caravane stays in Mauritania.
Nomad income stays pitifully low.

Here it is in spades. Who could benefit more from a more
integrated world than the Mauritanian nomads? Better off as
camel herders, you say? Perhaps, but tell them that when they
lack money to buy sick children medicine, or send them to
school. And yet the global institutions we have in place in this
world of 'globalisation' prevent the Mauritanians from participating, simply because they live on the wrong side of the fence.

From Fujita and Abeiderrahmane's stories we understand that
globalisation is about trade. But, crucially, it is about the spoils
of that trade, and how they are divided.

Trade wars

Trade, say the economists, is a good thing. According to basic
economic theory, countries that specialise in what they are good
at and then trade with others will be better off. Australia, for
instance, is rich because we dig up and export our natural
resources, and grow great swathes of wheat and other agricultural commodities across our vast tracts of cheap land. We trade
this with, say, Asia for cheap clothes and running shoes made
with cheap labour. Everybody is better off because a greater
amount of commodities is produced. We have more clothes and
running shoes than we would if we made them ourselves, and
they are cheaper this way.

The figures back up the theory. In general, in the post-war world, countries that have freed up their economies carefully and selectively have reaped rewards. On the other hand, when countries put up barriers to trade, things go awry.

Broad trade trends corroborate economists' thinking about how trade benefits growth. The boom years of the late twentieth century that brought the rich countries so much growth was accompanied by an ever-increasing volume of world trade (see the chart below). At the same time, those countries that traded more freely with others saw their people—in terms of GDP per head—get richer faster. When countries stop trading, things go awry. In the Great Depression, when the US government put up high tariff barriers to protect its domestic industry, world trade suffered terribly, people en masse were unemployed, misery multiplied, and the foundations for the Second World War were laid.

So far so simple.

Or is it? The post-war world as a whole may have grown in line with the volume of trade but, as we saw in the 'People, people, people . . .' chapter, the rewards of that growth were

A trader's era—world GDP and trade, 1950–2002

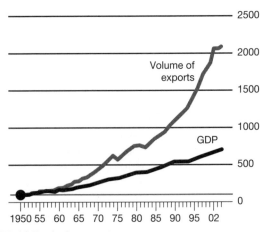

Source: World Trade Organization.

somewhat unevenly distributed. The reason? Free trade policies in the rich countries were introduced only after their industries were strong enough to take it. In the 'Money and work' chapter we saw that, throughout the nineteenth century, one by one countries took off on the road to economic modernisation. The common link between these countries was their fierce protection of industries while they were developing.

Britain is portrayed as the bastion of nineteenth-century *laissez faire*, market-led economics, but this was only after centuries of fierce protectionism—high tariffs and prohibition on foreign goods—had installed the country's industries at the top of the global tree. Britain's history of protectionism began as far back as the fourteenth century, when Edward II brought Flemish weavers into the country and banned the import of woollen cloth. At the turn of the eighteenth century, Britain banned wool imports from Ireland and calico from India, destroying their industries.

America slapped tariffs of up to 50 per cent on manufactured imported goods through the nineteenth century, only dropping them in 1913. They rose to 37 per cent in 1922, and in the Depression went as high as 48 per cent. Protectionism was a critical contributor to the American Civil War—high tariffs helped the northern states, but hurt the Confederacy. When the North won, the country hiked import taxes as high as they had ever been. America's professed devotion to free trade—and a wobbly devotion it is—flies in the face of its own economic history.

Even in Asia, where the economic miracles of the twentieth century pulled Japan, Taiwan and South Korea out of poverty, it has been because they protected key industries and actively promoted exports, allowing imports in only when their own industries had become world leaders.

So the argument that free trade is the only way for countries to develop is clearly bogus. But even if it weren't, politicians tend to be less enthusiastic about trade than economists because they have to be careful about their voters' jobs.

If they get carried away with liberalising trade—even if according to their economic advisers everybody will be better off in the long run because of it—they may find that a big clothes factory in their constituency has been forced to close down, putting 3000 of their constituents out of work. Next election, they're out of a job.

It's not just jobs, either. Trade has implications for the environment, for culture and for the way societies work, all of which politicians have a keen sensitivity to. Unlike economists, politicians see trade as a zero-sum game—they will only open their own markets in exchange for others opening theirs. The big trick for a trade negotiator is to get other countries to open up their markets without giving anything at all away. The EU's refusal to let Tiviski market camel's cheese pales into insignificance against the US$352 billion of subsidies the rich world pays its farmers directly each year.

To cite just one example, in 2001 alone the US handed $3.4 billion in subsidies to its cotton farmers—just 25 000 of them, each already worth on average $800 000. US cotton subsidies brought the worldwide prices of cotton down by an estimated 25 per cent, felt most keenly by those who could least afford it—clearly not US farmers but those in Africa and other

---

Dinner party factlets

- Rich countries give their farmers nearly US$1 billion a day—six times what they give poor countries in aid.
- The EU spends US$1.6 billion on beet sugar subsidies, and over US$5 billion on price support (Australia is sueing in the WTO).
- Bangladesh pays the US more than US$300 million a year to sell its clothes in North America.
- Rich countries impose trade barriers four times higher on poor countries' products than other rich countries' products, worth US$700 billion a year to the poor.

countries where cotton farming provides a close to subsistence living. In Europe, the US and Australia, agriculture employs barely a fraction of the population, while in the poorest countries farmers make up nearly three quarters of the working population. If those farmers could get hold of just a few of the benefits available from free trade, what a difference it would make to the issues we saw in the 'People, people, people . . .' chapter. But, as the camel milkers will witness, the rich world is far from relinquishing its iron grip on the world trading regime.

Out of such simple conflicts, big wars grow. As globalisation speeds up as we head deeper into Crunch Time, there is little hope that this will change. On the contrary, the game is getting nastier.

Some very Crunch Time trade disputes

Non a McMerde, 1999: The US wanted Europe to allow imports of beef injected with growth hormones. The EU said no: hormone injections cause cancer in children. The WTO said 'rubbish', and gave America permission to slap tariffs on European goods in retaliation. America did, charging European exporters of luxury goods, motorcycles and foodstuffs some $300 million to bring their goods into the country. One of the European farmers affected by 100 per cent trade tax was Jose Bove, a left-leaning Frenchman who produced Roquefort cheese. In retaliation, Bove smashed up a local McDonald's, causing US$250 000 of damage and turning himself into a national anti-capitalist hero. Ironically, though, his protest was *for* free trade—particularly in respect to Roquefort cheese—not against it.

Tripsed out, 2001: Multinationals in rich countries are peeved that their valuable patents, which protect their ideas and products, are easily trodden on in poor countries. Copies of everything from the latest Microsoft application through to Gucci handbags and HIV drugs pour out of the developing world. American pharmaceutical companies estimate they lose some US$500 million in India alone through patent infringement. So they made all the members of the

WTO sign on to Trips (Trade-related aspects of Intellectual Property Rights) in 1994, with poor countries signing because they thought that in return rich countries might concede on agricultural tariffs and subsidies. How wrong they were.

Trips lays down a long list of rules for the kind of protection countries should provide to patent holders. These protections can be fiercely expensive. America, for example, has a patent office with an annual budget of US$1 billion and a staff of more than 3000 highly trained scientists, engineers and lawyers. Most poor countries will at best have a dozen patent officers. For the developing countries, the cost of bringing their systems up to scratch is estimated to be in the millions of dollars—money that might be better spent elsewhere. The issue came to a head when America threatened to sue Brazil in the WTO for allowing the production of generic versions of HIV antivirals. But Brazil retaliated by invoking a clause in the Trips agreement which allows patent infringement 'in the face of a national emergency or other circumstances of extreme urgency'. It had a case because the US was busy producing massive amounts of Cipro, a German drug used as an anti-anthrax agent, after a lunatic sent envelopes of the deadly virus in the post to American politicians. In the end the US backed down, and allowed Brazil to produce HIV drugs.

One lump or two?

When the Howard government first considered a free trade agreement (FTA) between the US and Australia, it commissioned a report on the potential economic benefits from the Centre for International Economics, a Canberra-based think-tank. According to the report, the biggest constituency to benefit from such an agreement would be sugar growers, who could expect extra exports worth US$442 million if they were given full access to the American market.

When the FTA was finally unveiled in February 2004, the sugar industry was the only major area which was specifically excluded. Under the terms of the deal, American companies can flood Australian markets with agricultural goods, films and television programs, cars and the rest. But Australian sugar farmers (who can't survive without government handouts and have received three federal government rescue packages in six years) can't access the American market. Why?

The US sugar industry is hopelessly uneconomic. The American government pays its sugar growers more than twice the world price for their crops, an annual handout of US$1.6 billion. According to the US General Accounting Office, the high price of sugar costs American consumers $2 billion a year in higher food prices. But the sugar industry is highly politically sensitive, in the US as well as Australia. The biggest sugar growing state in the US, Florida, was the state that handed the presidency to George W. Bush by less than a whisker. Opening America's sugar markets to Australian competition under an FTA was not an option for 'free-trader' Bush.

This left Mr Howard in something of a sensitive political position. His government, due for a general election some time in 2004, held four sugar seats by margins of 3 per cent or less. How could he save face with the temperamental sugar growers? Answer: money. In April he announced yet another package of payments (read bribes) to sugar growers, $444 million of taxpayers' money in compensation for his failure in negotiations with America. But, when the handouts were announced, the FTA had yet to even be ratified by either the Americans or the Australians, and even if it had, it wouldn't have harmed the sugar growers—it just wouldn't have done them any good either.

Take that, capitalist scum!

It already seems a long time ago, but at the turn of the millennium it looked as if global capitalism's glaring faults had created enormous momentum for change. Remember the anti-globalisation riots?

TV images showed tens of thousands of protesters converging upon the World Trade Organization talks in Seattle, and the G8 summit in Genoa disappeared beneath clouds of CS gas. The protestors were made up of all sorts of different people pushing all sorts of different causes—trade unionists claiming that globalisation destroys jobs, environmentalists complaining that globalisation destroys trees, rioters against GM-foods or dolphin-killing tuna nets, development lobbies such as Oxfam shouting that poor countries are being dealt a lousy hand by the global trade system, consumer groups shouting about the loss of choice and the corporate takeover of our lives—you name it, they were there.

It was amazing and encouraging. No one could object to the activists' compassion for the world's poor, the environment and the workers of the world who were being given the raw prawn by the elite that run global power politics. For many, us included, the instinct was to cheer on the civil action and encourage the nascent 'global justice' movement. On the other hand, there was one persistent niggling question: What is it that these people actually want? Do they want to stop trade, abolish private property, and restrict the very freedoms that allow us to protest at all?

Twenty-first century issues are more complex and inter-connected than any we have encountered before, because everybody involved in the interaction is right, and everybody is wrong. The vast majority of the protesters in Seattle were not there fighting for a return to Soviet-style communism or state control of resources. Instead, the WTO had become the magnet for a myriad of often-contradictory complaints about the ills of globalisation. And there is truth and error in all the protesters' claims. The fact is that because the world is now a faster, riskier, more contagious place, the 'unintended consequences' of capitalism become apparent violently, critically and very quickly. And it is these unintended consequences that

> Is there anything more ridiculous in the news today than the protests against the World Trade Organization in Seattle? . . . [the protestors are] a Noah's ark of flat-earth advocates, protectionist trade unions and yuppies looking for their 1960s fix.
>
> Thomas Friedman, *New York Times*

bring the educated middle classes out onto the streets to be baton-charged and tear gassed.

So what were they protesting against? Many would simply label it the 'Washington Consensus', after the Washington-based global economic institutions—the WTO, the IMF and the World Bank—which together have decided on a particular type of economic program for the world. One which many don't agree with. The Washington Consensus is how the winners see the world economy. It's doing very nicely, thank you. Helping us grow. Putting more cigars in our walk-in humidors and toys in our kids' bedrooms. So let's have more of the same— more openness, more freedom, more trade. Critics call it

---

What don't we want?
Neo-liberalism!
When don't we want it?
Ever!

Neo-liberalism is what anti-globalists call the tough side of free-market economics. In *Take it Personally*, radical businesswoman Dame Anita Roddick defines its manifesto as:

- **The rule of the market** liberating 'free' enterprise from any bonds imposed by the government no matter how much social damage this causes.
- **Cutting public expenditure for social services** such as education and health care and water supply, all in the name of reducing government's role.
- **Deregulation** of laws that could reduce profits, including measures to protect workers and the environment.
- **Privatisation** by selling state-owned enterprises, goods and services to private investors. Although done in the name of greater efficiency, which is often needed, privatisation concentrates wealth into fewer hands and makes the public pay more.
- **Eliminating the concept of 'the Public Good'** and replacing it with 'individual responsibility'. Pressuring the poorest people to find solutions to their lack of health care, education and social security and branding them, if they fail, as 'lazy'.

'neo-liberalism'—and they're not talking liberal in a pot smoking, hippy kind of a way. They're talking about *laissez faire* liberals from 200 years ago who thought business should be free to do whatever it wanted, because business creates wealth. Neo-liberalism, shout the protestors, is gospel at the World Bank and the IMF (institutions that were originally created to help eradicate poverty and encourage growth). It means they support the economic status quo, however unfair, and force poor countries to open themselves up to cut-throat competition. They make weak governments pursue policies that promote these goals no matter what the environmental or social costs.

Whether or not you agree completely with her wording and tone, Dame Anita Roddick pretty much captures the main thrust of the economic policies pushed by the IMF, in both the developed and developing worlds (see box on page 207). The initial results have, in some cases, been a great boost to growth. But as we have turned the corner into Crunch Time, the results have been not so good. It is time for a new paradigm, say the anti-globalisation protesters.

'Hang on a minute,' say the Washington types, putting down their cigars and loosening their watch chains. 'The world is a complicated place, and when you mess with it the results are unpredictable and chaotic. The best way to avoid chaos and to encourage investment and economic activity is to interfere with things as little as possible—let market forces work their magic. Economic stability and trade liberalisation help growth, and growth is good.'

'What's more,' the statisticians say, 'it's working.'

According to the World Bank, between 1990 and 1999 the percentage of the world's people living in absolute poverty fell by 6 per cent. But World Bank figures have been proven somewhat dubious (see box on page 209). Despite this, one thing is for sure: the anti-globalisation protesters are right in claiming neo-liberal policies, combined with the speed, contagion and risk of the Crunch Time world, have boosted the

Lies, damned lies and statistics

World Bank figures on the number of poor in this world get quoted
with great gusto on both sides of the debate. For example, the neo-
liberals often use them to prove the point that, ugly as some of the
global economy's characteristics may be, the existing model is
helping the world's poor. Between 1990 and 1999, the World Bank
claimed the percentage of the people living in absolute poverty fell
from 29 to 23 per cent.

But don't believe everything (anything?) you read.

According to a recent paper by Columbia University academics
Sanjay Reddy, an economist, and philosopher Thomas Pogge, the
methodology the World Bank uses is flawed and unscientific. The
1.2 billion number 'calculated' by the World Bank, 'down to the last
10 000', might as well have been plucked from the air. It doesn't even
contain figures from China or India, the two poorest and most
populous countries in the world. And the apparent downward trend
in this number is a result of the way it is compiled, not the result of
an actual decrease in poverty.

Source: http://www.columbia.edu/~sr793/povpop.pdf.

'unintended consequences' of capitalism—things such as the
winner-takes-all syndrome, increasing instability and environmental and social destruction. How do we know all this? Well,
let's look at an example: the global financial system—that
edifice of rules, institutions and speculation which provides the
lubrication for the machine of real economic growth around the
world.

Money, money, money . . . it's a rich man's world

Money markets are the on-track betting agents in the world's
economic racecourse. Trading floors even used to look like
the bookies ring at the Royal Randwick. Only 2 per cent of the

US$1.5 trillion worth of international currency that swills around the world every day is *not* some kind of gamble.

Most of this money is governed by rich people or rich institutions that bet on whether the euro will be worth more tomorrow than the dollar relative to today's figure, or whether the pound will be worth more than the Swedish krone, or whatever. This isn't entirely because bankers and finance types like a flutter. The money is genuinely needed to oil the wheels of growth.

Global capital markets provide 'liquidity'. This means that when those with cash think there's money to be made by investing in an opportunity overseas, there are people out there willing to provide local funds in exchange for foreign money. Without this liquidity, opportunities would be lost. At the same time, globalisation has amplified the impact of money movements on decisions at all levels, from paying the household bills to international debt negotiations. In the interconnected, competitive global economy, with money hopping borders more easily than rain clouds, the people we have elected to actually run our countries are sidelined as international capital markets rampage over their economies.

Deregulated banking systems, money sloshing around the globe, the increasingly large amounts of borrowed money at the disposal of financiers, not to mention hedge funds and the odd billionaire investor, have all had two fundamental consequences

---

Dinner party factlets:

- US$1.5 trillion passes through the international currency market every day.
- That's 30 times the GDP of the entire developed world put together.
- 98 per cent of that cash is 'on-track' betting on the world economy.

> Just as capitalism creates winner-take-all societies, glob-
> alisation, is creating a winner-take-all world.
>
> Karl Marx didn't say this, but he might have
> if he were alive today

for the world's economies. On the one hand, economies which have 'opened up' can see rapid benefits in terms of economic growth and international competitiveness. They become more attractive for the global investors and can attract investment capital and factories more easily than others. This puts pressure on all economies to globalise and liberalise, to take advantage of incoming cash.

On the other hand, 'opening up' an economy means taking away the controls and regulations that stopped large amounts of money from leaving it in a hurry—'capital flight'. What this means is that when a country has a domestic economic 'event'—say, a run on a bank—globalisation means it rapidly comes to the attention of the international investment community, which demands higher interest rates on the cash it's lending because of increased risk. Higher payments make businesses fail, businesses fail and the currency collapses. So a domestic drama becomes an international crisis.

Don't collapse for me Argentina . . .

In 2001, Argentina's 'economic collapse' made world headlines. It was a direct result of the way capitalism is practised in the twenty-first century, combined with the nature of the world's attitude today. Argentina is a textbook example of the problems global capital flows can cause when the markets turn on you. Before things went belly up, Argentina was an IMF star. Under the leadership of President Carlos Menem it put its hand up to every globalised, liberal, free-market policy the IMF thrust upon it. The government pledged to keep the currency stable against the US dollar, and hyperinflation calmed down. It privatised everything in sight—ports, railroads, utilities, you name it—and in response, the country got rich. In the early to mid 1990s, it had the highest growth rate in South America.

Unfortunately, having allowed foreign cash to walk in freely, it found that the same cash could walk out again without even stopping to say 'adios'. The first signs of trouble came with a currency crisis in Mexico in 1995. Mexico devalued its peso. Devaluation scared international investors. They yanked their money from *all* of Latin America, Argentina included. The Argentines did their best—they reassured the international moneymen by keeping the exchange rate fixed. But the gap between the interest payments foreign investors wanted on the money they'd poured into Argentina and what the Argentines could pay kept growing. The last straw came in 2001 when people thought the banks were going broke and tried to get their money out all at once.

The country defaulted on US$155 billion of public debt. The biggest belly-up in history. And it devalued its currency. Millions lost their savings and their homes, unable to make payments on US dollar mortgages. A quarter of the country was tossed out of work—unemployment in cities skyrocketed as high as 40 per cent—poverty became endemic, and income per person was halved in five years, putting Argentina about level with Botswana. No Argentine was left untouched by this crisis. All because nervous fund managers somewhere else squeezed Argentina too hard, then pulled their cash.

This sad story is repeated in many other countries on the periphery of western wealth, that is to say, in places where most of the world's people live. Huge gains and high growth have been followed by catastrophic crashes—look at east Asia in the late 1990s.

When domestic economic shocks hit, when fraud or bad debts weaken banks, what does the international investment community do? It flings gasoline on the flames by betting against countries in crisis and sticking investment cash on the first flight out. Remember the Washington Consensus? It says financial crises are short-term blips on the upward curve of global growth. The benefits of globalisation must override the inherent human desire for stability. Easy to say from an office suite overlooking Capitol Hill, perhaps. Not so easy in a sewerless barrio. The rewards for globalisation are an offer that can't be refused, but at the same time we find ourselves at the whim of the fickle winds of financial fate. High rewards, high risks—it's the nature of our times.

There is one man who would be desperately disappointed to see the way things have turned out for the international institutions—but probably not desperately surprised. In the 'Money and work' chapter we quote how he thought we were all semipathological, semi-criminals for working more than 15 hours a week. Britain's great economic genius, John Maynard Keynes, was a key designer of the world's post-war institutions, and his story demonstrates clearly how, in human affairs, might is clearly more important than right.

Imperial preference

Great Britain at the end of 1940 had been chased out of mainland Europe via an evacuation of 300 000 men at Dunkirk. It was facing the Italian army in North Africa, and it was reliant, as ever, for food and industrial supplies via sea—a supply threatened by Nazi Germany's submarine fleet. To add to its woes, the British were broke. In the third quarter of 1940 alone, the country lost close to £700 million, and at this rate it would be completely bankrupt by the end of the year. On 8 December, Prime Minister Winston Churchill sent a desperate but dignified letter to US President Franklin Roosevelt, recuperating from his election victory in the Caribbean aboard the US Navy's *Tuscaloosa*, beseeching him for help. Churchill, who was no mean letter writer, described it as 'one of the most important I ever wrote'. By his own account Roosevelt read and reread it for two days, sitting on his deckchair, eventually coming to a decision. Just as a neighbour would lend a friend a hose to put out a house fire, America would lend Britain the tools it needed to put out the fire consuming Europe.

Britain, as Churchill had put it, was America's first line of defence against the Axis in both Europe and the Pacific, and Roosevelt knew he couldn't let the country be defeated. At the same time, he didn't like Britain's empire or anything it stood for. America might have invaded its neighbours on a regular basis, but Roosevelt drew a distinction. 'The colonial system means war,' he once told his son. 'Exploit the resources of an India, a Burma, a Java; take all the wealth out of those countries but never put anything back . . . all you're doing is storing up the kind of trouble that leads to war.' Stopping over in Gambia en route to a conference in Casablanca, Roosevelt remarked that for every dollar the British put into the country,

---

The fortune teller

I can see vast changes coming over a now peaceful world; great upheavals, terrible struggles; wars such as one cannot imagine; and I tell you London will be in danger—London will be attacked and I shall be very prominent in the defence of London . . . I see further ahead than you do. I see into the future. The country will be subjected somehow to a tremendous invasion . . . but I tell you I shall be in command of the defences of London and I shall save London and the Empire from disaster.

Winston Churchill, age 16
speaking to a classmate at school in 1892

it had taken ten out. 'It's just plain exploitation,' he said. More than this, the British imperial system was an offence against the 'liberal' trading order that America wanted for the world.

In 1932 Britain, suffering from the effects of the Great Depression and responding to America's Smoot-Hawley Act which restricted trade, introduced 'imperial preference'—preferential tariffs for colonial products, effectively an imperial trade bloc. America was not a part of this 'preference'. So when Roosevelt decided that America was to lend its garden hose to Churchill to help put out the fires of Europe, he had one eye on defending democracy and the other, some might say, on breaking open the imperial markets for America's goods.

America's assistance was provided under a program of Lend-Lease—in other words, America gave Britain arms and ships and planes and things to use against the Nazis, on the understanding that somehow America would get payment for them at some time—to be specified—in the future. As Britain's chief negotiator, Keynes—despite suffering badly from heart disease which had already put him at death's door—ploughed back and forth across the Atlantic four times during the course of the war to settle the terms.

Keynes may have been a genius but he was in no position to negotiate. Britain was over a barrel. 'The US administration was very careful to take every possible precaution to see that the British were as near as possible bankrupt before any assistance was given', he wrote. The biggest sticking point was Article VII of the Lend-Lease agreement:

> The terms and conditions upon which the United Kingdom receives defence aid from the United States . . . shall provide against discrimination in either the United States of America or the United Kingdom against the importation of any produce originating in either country.

In other words, a free trade agreement between the two countries that would tear up imperial preference. Keynes saw free trade wiping away British industry as American goods flooded the country, and what remained of Britain's cash flowed unopposed across the Atlantic. But in the end, Britain needed money desperately, and the Americans were willing to provide it—on their terms. As the British got further and further into hock as the war progressed, its position on other issues, like Keynes' heart, became weaker and weaker.

A hotel in New Hampshire

Keynes saw some things clearly: whatever happened, at the end of the war Britain would be up to its neck in debt, and it would be heavily dependent on expensive imports to rebuild itself. The problem with this situation—high debt, lousy terms of trade—is that in a system of free trade and money movements it simply compounds itself. Debt repayments mount up, and there is little money left over to invest in ways of creating better products to improve the terms of trade. In other words, post-war Britain would be in the same situation as many 'Highly Indebted Poor Countries' are at the beginning of the twenty-first century.

In September 1941, having come back from Washington after the first Article VII negotiations, Keynes sat down to create a grand design that would help stop this vicious circle from turning. His plan, the International Clearing Union (ICU), would encourage countries which had provided loans (mostly the US) to adjust their terms of trade by charging them interest on their trade surpluses. A plan which placed restrictions on the world's strongest players? Which redistributed cash from the rich to the poor? Clearly a non-starter.

Keynes plan was put up against that of America's economic policy genius of the Second World War—Harry Dexter White. White was a straight-laced Treasury department mandarin, short and stocky with a trim moustache and, remarkably, a communist spy who was passing information through to the

> I sympathise with those who would minimise, rather than maximise, economic entanglements between nations. Ideas, knowledge, art, hospitality, travel—these are things which should of their nature be international. But let goods be homespun whenever it is reasonably and conveniently possible; and, above all, let finance be primarily national.
>
> J.M. Keynes, 1933
> 'National Self-Sufficiency' in *The Collected Writings of John Maynard Keynes*, vol. 21, Donald Moggeridge ed., London, Macmillan and Cambridge University

Russians on a regular basis. His attitude to Keynes's plan: 'We have been perfectly adamant on that point. We have taken the position of absolutely no, on that.'

White's equivalent of the ICU was the International Stabilization Fund, designed to maintain currency stability, reduce foreign exchange controls and lend money to countries in trouble. When real negotiations over the shape of the post-war world began at Bretton Woods in July 1944, it was the only plan left on the table. The International Stabilization Fund became the International Monetary Fund, and it was determined that the IMF would be governed by a complex voting arrangement based largely on the economic power of countries at the end of the war. 'The US,' decided White, 'should have enough votes to block any decision.' The IMF and its sister institution the World Bank would be located in Washington—thus was born the Washington Consensus.

International conspiracy

'So globalisation is a grand American conspiracy to kick the rest of the world while it's down?' Mike asked.

'Not really,' replied Adrian.

After the negotiations, Keynes conceded in a letter to *The Times* that some of the policies agreed at Bretton Woods 'may . . . be very foolish' and 'destructive of international trade'. But the way the Washington institutions were, and the way that the post-war world has developed, tell two different stories. On the one hand, America undoubtedly wanted the world built to its own design, and it has done a lot of godawful things in the half century in which it has ruled the roost. It is arrogant and self interested and all those things. But at the same time, look at what has happened in the world since the end of the Second World War. In 1945, America was even more pre-eminent than it is now with Japan and Europe laid to waste. Rather than grind those countries into the dust, America helped them create democracies and build up their economies—to build markets for its own products no doubt—but nonetheless, powerful as it is at the moment, it's nothing like it was fifty years ago.

Into the twenty-first century, too, America's own growth and stability relies on the growth and stability of the whole world. But that doesn't mean that powerful players won't always want to tilt the playing field in their direction.

Globalisation, we concluded, is a two-way street—although

If you believe that if we all just love each other more, there'll be a transformation of consciousness and no one will ever oppress other people again, then I am wasting your time, and so are you.

George Monbiot
writing in a *Manifesto for a New World Order*

It's a little bit embarrassing to have been concerned with the human problem all one's life and find at the end that one has no more to offer than 'try to be a little kinder'.

Aldous Huxley

the contrast between Den Fujita's success in Japan and Nancy Abeiderrahmane's failure in Mauritania doesn't make it look that way . . . at first glance. But the stories don't end there.

Den Fujita retired as chairman and chief executive of McDonald's Japan in March 2003, just as the company slipped into the red to the tune of US$20 million. Japan's economic woes, combined with a series of protests against the fast-food chain's meat handling and animal rights record, forced the company to cut prices to such an extent that it was pretty much making a loss on every burger it sold. Because they were so cheap—and, at the end of a ten-year recession, people were feeling so poor—they did sell a lot of them. The company tried all sorts of other tactics to dig itself out of the mud, broadening the menu, changing its advertising but, say commentators, the company may just be a victim of a more powerful force than globalisation: fashion. Speaking to website Japan Inc., 18-year-old Ken Ogawa said:

> It used to be McDonald's every evening after school, but not now. We used to drink coffee, or maybe eat something, but the main thing was knowing that everyone would be there. McDonald's just isn't somewhere we want to meet any more.

As for Abeiderrahmane . . . at the time of writing it looked to be several more years before she would be successful in accessing the wealthy western markets with her camel's cheese. Her attitude, however, is best summed up by the sign on her office wall: 'Don't EVER give up'. Good advice, perhaps, for all of us as we head deeper into Crunch Time.

9
CONCLUSION

Way back in the Introduction, we quoted Bobby Kennedy:

> Few will have the greatness to bend history, but each of us can work to change a small portion of events, and in the total of all those acts will be written the history of this generation.

In that same speech in 1966, Bobby Kennedy popularised an ancient piece of eastern wisdom. Three years after his brother had been shot dead and a couple of years before he too suffered the same fate, Kennedy told his audience, 'There is a Chinese curse which says, "May he live in interesting times". Like it or not, we live in interesting times . . .'

Kennedy's short life may have been true to the curse, but the curse itself is based on a lie. Any Chinese speaker will confirm that there is no such curse in Chinese. It is a modern, western invention. Not Chinese, not ancient, but nonetheless resonating with an ironic wisdom that sounds like it's been around forever. It is a great metaphor for understanding Crunch Time. If ever there were interesting times, these are they.

We live in interesting times, but so what, hasn't everybody from the dawn of history? Why is the twenty-first century any more serious, critical, or even interesting than those that have come before?

Having been through this journey, we offer four reasons why now is different, why the twenty-first century will suffer from the Chinese curse more than any that came before it. Today the world is a faster, more contagious, riskier and more fragile place. These are the fundamental factors that make our time more critical for the future than any that has come before.

Stop the world, I want to get off

Remember Archbishop Wulfstan a thousand years ago admonishing his Viking-ravaged flock with the gloomy words, 'The world is in a rush, and is getting closer to its end'. How would he feel now? Crunch Time accelerates every day. Change happens faster, innovation happens faster, knowledge develops and obsolesces faster, decisions are made faster, and their consequences—intended and unintended—become clearer in a shorter time span. And these consequences shape and surround our lives. They influence the way we live, the values we hold dear and the relationships we form. They matter to the permanence and credibility of the institutions around us that provide support, structure and work, including families, employers and governments.

You don't have to be a genius to see this. Over the course of the hundred years to now, the developed world has seen improvements in transport (from horse and cart and steam train to mass jet travel and even space tourism), communications (from the telegraph to wireless radio to satellite television) and knowledge (from basic literacy as the minimum exception to mass higher education) which have simply made the world quicker.

The Wright Brothers made the first powered aeroplane flight at Kitty Hawk on 17 December 1903. It lasted 12 seconds and took them 120 feet (36.5 metres). By 1919, Australian Prime Minister Billy Hughes was offering a massive cash prize to anyone who could fly from Britain to the great southern continent in less than 30 days. Half a dozen people died trying. Now the journey takes less than a day, and a couple of thousand of us will probably be making it every day with nary a casualty (the occasional case of deep vein thrombosis aside).

In the middle of the nineteenth century, Massachusetts portrait painter Samuel Morse tapped out, 'What hath God wrought?' in the first-ever telegraph message. The code Morse invented carried a thin stream of messages that brought instant communication over long distances. That code officially disappeared a few months before this century opened. Today, in place of a series of dots and dashes, we have ones and zeros digitally relaying simulcasts of rock concerts, the Olympics, live terrorist attacks and firefights watched by millions, even billions, all over the world. These events are carried by communications satellites orbiting the earth. The very first began circling back in 1969. Now hundreds of them criss-cross the heavens, littering the skies like discarded crisp packets at an amusement park.

Another (already) overused statistic: it took 40 years for radio in the United States to gain an audience of 50 million. That's the same number of people who were using the personal computer 15 years after it hit production. For the same number to be regularly using the Internet? Four years.

As for knowledge, we're told that at the beginning of the twenty-first century it is the single most important industrial sector in the developed world. In 1900, the overwhelming majority of people in developed countries worked with their hands. They were farm-workers, builders, factory hands, miners or servants. By the 1950s, that figure had dropped to about half in the US labour force. Now, less than a quarter of America's workers make their living from any type of manual work. The same is becoming true in the rest of the developed world—more and more people are working in the amorphous world of bits, rather than the more concrete world of atoms, and it matters.

Over the course of the last decade, the addition of one further critical factor has accentuated this trend: communications technology. Email and the Internet have pushed the ride even faster. The network created by a global web of email addresses and servers has simply revved up the pace of life by increasing the amount of communications and information available to each and every one of us. It is a faster world for us, and in a globalised world that means it is a faster world for everybody. We saw in 'Science' how information technology and communications are driving the exponential growth of scientific knowledge, and what it means for us.

These three forces—transport, communications and knowledge—have conspired to up the pace on the global treadmill from a gentle jog through to a competitive sprint. The world economy is not only faster; it is faster for just about everyone who is engaged with it.

It's catching

In these interesting times, the world is a fiercely contagious place.

A few months into the year 2000, a small group of truck drivers and farmers angered by fuel hikes in the United Kingdom began a movement that copied protests (about something completely different) they'd seen by French farmers on TV.* As other angry motorists in Britain saw the fuel protests on TV, they too joined in. The popular uprising came close to bringing the world's fourth biggest economy to a grinding halt.

A few months earlier, an international collection of misfits with barely a goal in common but a shared antipathy towards free trade and the World Trade Organization created such violence and confusion in the streets of Seattle that one of

---

* They gathered en masse on the country's roads and blocked access to petrol distribution centres.

global politics' dullest events became a symbol of the bank-ruptcy of world governance. Masked, black-clad riot policemen took to the streets for subsequent meetings and clashes in Prague, Genoa, Melbourne—anywhere, in fact, where the global elite meet—generating an as yet unfinished ritual of trans-national repression and resistance. And it's not just a street phenomenon. Contagion can arrive at your desktop.

In 1999, a bored computer programmer from New Jersey developed and distributed a small software package he'd been working on: the Melissa virus. Estimates of the damage this caused come in at around US$80 million. That is small beer compared to the handiwork of MafiaBoy, a 16-year-old from a genteel suburb of Montreal who broke into computer networks around the world, from Denmark to South Korea. At MafiaBoy's court hearing, experts estimated the young man had been responsible for damage, lost business and costs of US$1.7 billion. From his bedroom, all by himself. Quite an achievement.

In the economic arena, this new kind of contagion is well documented. It is a vicious cycle that plays itself out over and over again: Mexico's currency crisis, Black Monday, Russia, Asia, LTCM, Argentina, the stock market crash of mid-2002. In a world of huge capital, technology and trade flows, it is no surprise that stock markets and general economic conditions have a greater level of interconnection between countries and regions. Yet in times of crisis, those connections just get closer.

Protests, computer bugs and investor confidence may be contagious, but it seems diseases are more contagious these days. During the past decades scientists have discovered pre-viously unknown infectious diseases for which there is no effective treatment at the rate of one a year. HIV is the most spectacular example. Unheard of before the 1980s, it has now killed millions worldwide. SARS, a respiratory virus, brought South-East Asia to a screeching halt at the beginning of 2003. Over the next few months, the illness spread to more than two dozen countries in North America, South America, Europe and

Asia. It was brought under control by isolating patients and finding a treatment, but it was one of half a dozen outbreaks in the previous five years.

Diseases enjoy the travel benefits of globalisation as much as humans do. The Black Death spread through the medieval world in ships. The Ebola virus skipped from an African village to a German isolation ward in a single plane ride. Air travel carried the insects that brought West Nile Fever to the United States. In 1998–99 a virus combined with an outbreak of Japanese Swine Fever killed hundreds in Malaysia, the epidemic striking just ten miles from Kuala Lumpur's new international airport. Each of these health catastrophes was averted only through late intervention, when doctors arrived from America's Centre for Disease Control in Atlanta, Georgia. They flew in.

In early 2002 in the UK, a new government agency was unveiled to manage and combat the spread of infectious diseases. It was needed, said the government's top medical adviser, because diseases have become tougher and tougher to detect and monitor. His reasons included big increases in world travel, new technology-related illnesses, global warming, changing sexual behaviour and new drug-resistant organisms.

So Crunch Time is a contagious time, and that makes it interesting. But interesting times aren't necessarily bad times. Knowledge, understanding, culture, the finer things in life cross borders as easily as germs.

At the time of writing, one of Mike's close friends was having a bone marrow transplant to treat his cancer. The bone marrow was flown from Spain to Sydney, the closest match they could find.

In the 1950s neither of our native lands were famous for their food—stodgy bland muck and a meat pie if you were lucky. Now lunchtime is a smorgasbord of the world's cuisine. The benefits of this aren't limited to us lucky diners. Restaurateurs have built themselves better lives on the back of this cultural exchange.

The frenzy of creativity that surrounded the dot.com boom—short-lived and unprofitable as it may have been—demonstrated that the Internet was still capable of spreading knowledge, as well as viruses, faster and further than at any other time in history. Despite the investment crash, we now buy our weekly shopping, books and holidays online efficiently and cheaply. The 'Science' chapter showed clearly how the contagion of ideas promises a cascade of ground-shaking technological innovation across the globe.

What all of the above examples illustrate is that we are now living in a world where everything from political movements, economic trends, fashion, communications and disease operate at a higher level of contagion. They spread faster and fartherer than ever before. When the US sneezed following 9/11, the rest of the world caught a cold. Why? Because communications, information technology, globalisation and liberalisation have created a world that is much more interconnected. These things spread like forest fires. And as the people of South-East Asia know, the smoke from raging wildfires can choke cities thousands of miles away for months.

Lady Luck's golden age

Our Chinese curse manifests itself in other ways too. There are objective reasons to believe the world we live in is riskier than it has ever been before, for the individual, for organisations, and for nation states. What does it mean to be riskier? It means that when things go well, they can go very, very well, very, very quickly—the dot.com boom showed us how the modern world can offer a huge upside to those in the right place at the right time with the right ideas. But when things go bad, they go rotten (ask a dot.com millionaire struggling to pay off the mortgage he took out at the height of the boom).

Look at the global insurance industry—global capital's

warehouse for risk. It is in a serious crisis that has been growing since the beginning of the 1990s. Hurricane Andrew, which hit Florida in summer 1992, was far and away the costliest loss the insurance industry had ever seen—US$18 billion. The two airplanes that hit the World Trade Center on September 11, 2001 cost US$70 billion. Before Andrew, insurers had assumed worst-case losses from a hurricane to be US$8 billion. They came up with that assumption when Hurricane Hugo hit Florida in 1989. Hugo cost a mere US$5.4 billion but took out several big insurers almost immediately. Hurricane Mireille in Japan in 1991 came in at US$6.5 billion—US$8 billion just seemed like the next plot on the graph.

Insurance is more than just a convenience—it is the grease that lubricates capitalism. In the wake of September 11, as insurers folded or stopped insuring stuff, all over the western world the fabric of daily life was slowly unravelling as small businesses from retail malls through to tour outlets were forced to close because they couldn't find insurance. Post–9/11 premium hikes affected pretty much every business on the face of the planet. In the face of multi-million dollar liability risks, airplanes stopped flying, manufacturers stopped making things, people's daily lives were affected in the most fundamental ways. These things matter.

The world in which we live is now more concentrated and interconnected—in terms of wealth, population and economic and social activity—than ever before. The reason why Hurricane Andrew was such a disaster was because lots and lots of rich people were clustered together in one part of the world, and when Andrew hit the impact on those people and what they owned was enormous. In the few blocks around the World Trade Center, the same was true.

The financial markets, too, are suffering from this new riskiness. Share prices have become more and more volatile—the riskiness of the world's top-four share markets steadily increased over the last twenty years of last century. Because of contagion they move together, so when one plunges it infects all the others. More than that, not only do stock markets move more closely together these days, they matter more. Worldwide, stock market capitalisation counts for more as a proportion of world GDP than it ever has before. Between March 2000 and March 2001, US$10 trillion of paper wealth was destroyed. That was nearly a third of world GDP. Never has so much been lost in such a short time.

This increased level of risk is driven by two things. As we saw in 'Globalisation', in the financial world it is driven by an increasing separation between what is happening in the real world and what is happening in the fictional world of money. But as we saw in the 'Environment' chapter, risks to our life and health are partly driven by the fact that we live at the end of nature—our surrounding material environment is almost entirely the product of human intervention. Think about it. Of the many things you have done since you got up this morning, how many could you honestly describe as being 'natural' to an animal species such as *Homo sapiens sapiens*? Probably just the basics. Perhaps this is not unique to our times and our lifestyles, but who could argue that in recent decades we have not moved ever further from nature towards a lifestyle wholly devised by ourselves?

So we are living in a world that is faster, more contagious, and extremely volatile. For us, that combination spells trouble. But that is not all.

This side up

We live in a fast, contagious and risky world, and there is little anyone can do to tame it. The world is more fragile than it has ever been. Everywhere you look, our public institutions—the government, democracy, international organisations—are seen as discredited, inadequate and simply not up to the job. As we saw in 'Globalisation', back in the last year of the Second World War the men who led world affairs (and men they were) firmly believed they could set in place institutions that would see the century out. The new American age was under-written at a series of meetings in a New Hampshire ski resort and a Georgetown mansion. Its results were the World Bank, the International Monetary Fund and the United Nations. Nation states were to be the building blocks of the *Pax Americana*. All would be good.

Along with the advances of the last part of the twentieth century, including information, communications, globalisation and liberalisation comes the understanding that human society and its interactions with the world in which we live are simply too complex to be governed effectively. Certainly at the global level, those institutions have proven to be incapable of addressing the challenges this new world has thrown at them. From military interventions in complex national conflicts such as Rwanda, Bosnia and Iraq, through to the complexities of global warming, population control and third world debt, they have all too often been accused of making things worse rather than better.

Until the end of the Cold War, the UN was considered a sterile but essentially harmless institution. Since then its ineffectiveness as a means of implementing American policy has led to it being side-lined by its sponsor and host nation. It still churns out study after study containing more and more statistics, but its concerns for the state of the world are only rivalled by the disregard of the world's most powerful states for its concerns. The conclusion of many is that the UN is a hollow talking shop.

The IMF and the World Bank too have failed to live up to their original promise. Their mandate when they were created in 1944 was to help prevent future conflicts by lending for reconstruction and development, and by smoothing out temporary balance of payments problems. They were to have no control over individual government's economic decisions nor did their mandate include a licence to intervene in national policy. Both now suffer from indelible and irreparable image problems (read faults). Critics say they are consistently used as a tool to promote western ideals and military causes; that because they serve the interests of their western masters, they can have little international legitimacy—but their money still talks.

In the sphere of economics, government after government has come a cropper after genuinely well-meaning attempts to manage boom followed by bust. But the problem has always been, and always will be, a lack of knowledge—the more we know, the more we know we don't know. Information about what is happening in an economy is approximate and always out of date; and the tools a government possesses to control economic activity are crude and brutish—taxation, spending, interest rates, currency circulation. Each of these takes a long and unpredictable amount of time to produce any effect, and the only genuinely discernible result of many economic management decisions is that—with hindsight—they appear to be exactly what wasn't needed at the time.

Politically, even when it is widely agreed what measures need to be taken to control particular risks or resolve certain issues, it's rare that the actual machinery of government will allow action to be taken. Look at the glacial progress that has been made towards achieving the environmental objectives agreed upon at the Rio Summit in 1992, and the hash up that was the Johannesburg Summit a decade later. The mismatch between local needs and international understanding and agreement is too wide to be bridged by our current institutions. Yet we're far from even beginning the process of redesigning the fragile governance structures that many would say are leading the world toward disaster.

Everywhere you look, the signs of fragile governance systems are showing through our social fabric. Witness the increase in numbers and power of non-governmental organisations from Greenpeace through to the US National Rifle Association. Not elected by anyone, yet increasingly responsible for influencing decisions and social standards. And look at the sharp and disturbing increase in the number of walled and gated communities—huge numbers of wealthy individuals in the United States and beyond who are using their purchasing power to remove themselves from society as a whole, creating a patchwork of suburban mini-states.

It's not all about you

The most difficult aspect of many of these issues and risks is that their causes are deeply embedded in the way we live—in what it means to be an active member of western society at the beginning of the twenty-first century. They cannot be isolated and extracted from the everyday actions of everyday people. If the simple act of driving to work in my new sports utility vehicle is a direct contributor to rising temperatures across the face of the earth, searching for solutions is often no less than a root and branch analysis of what it means to be a person.

Meanwhile, in searching for solutions, even if we knew everything there was to know about one specialisation, that wouldn't be enough. Poverty might be the result of poor economics, but it is also the result of different types of social interactions, cultural issues, or even physical processes such as transport, pollution, education and health. That is why so many of the sciences are at loggerheads with each other—look at the debates over the environment and economics, free trade and globalisation, security and freedom. Each of these, and the rest, are the result of serious disagreements between educated people with valid perspectives on a tangled world.

Perhaps it is this insight—that everything is connected and we are connected to everything—that has driven the increasing popularity of systems thinking. The twenty-first century will see huge growth in the study of complex systems in everything from management theory to cosmology. But at the same time, we can understand the persistence of religious beliefs and, in parallel, the rise of new age, holistic thinking.

Back to *Civilization* . . .

So we are entering a new phase of human evolution that is fundamentally different from all that has come before: we are victims of the Chinese curse. In Sid Meier's *Civilization* terms, just as players move from the Iron Age to the Middle Ages by developing construction and cartography, so we are moving from the Modern to the Post-Modern era (or from the Post-Modern to the Post-Post-Modern, or from the Post-Post Modern to the Post-Post-Post . . .) by developing science, communications and information technologies, and speeding globalisation.

We are not the first to observe this, by any means. Over twenty years ago Alvin Toffler, futurologist extraordinaire, said we are moving through the 'third wave' of change—the first wave was the agricultural revolution, the second wave the industrial revolution, and the third wave is the 'high speed' revolution. Controversial social scientist Manuel Castells now calls it the dawn of the 'network society'. Each of these and others contain within them a common core of insight and explanation. But individually they give us only a glimpse of how we should behave or how we should make decisions if we wish to both ride the waves of change and provide for a better future.

As players in our great game of civilisation, it is the decisions we make at this juncture, this turn, this roll of the dice that will determine whether we make it through to the next stage of the game; whether the passengers on Spaceship Earth have the food, water, shelter, resources, technology and spiritual substance to see our species through to the next stage of evolution.

It is Crunch Time.

It is complicated and brilliant. We are all micro-players in this macro-decision moment. It may be scary that there is no one individual that can do the work for us. There is no game designer to allow us to Ctrl-Alt-Del back to the start. On the other hand, there is a certain comfort in the knowledge that we cannot delegate, that every individual has the ability to move the world towards a better tomorrow. And if we have the ability, surely we have the obligation.

READINGS, REFERENCES AND RESOURCES

Here is a list of books and websites that we found useful putting this book together. It is not an exhaustive set of references or a categorised bibliography but a list of places to turn to if you want to get to know more about any of the subjects we have touched upon in this book.

General background

For general twenty-first century commentary and analysis, there is a burgeoning genre of books just like this one that look at general trends and make broad observations. Four of the best include:

- *Inevitable Surprises* by Peter Schwartz, published in Australia by Simon & Schuster, in which Californian futurologist Schwartz (he is perhaps more credible than this job description makes him sound) writes that the world is an unpredictable place, except that many things can be predicted, including: the death of retirement (in the rich west); lots of migration; a new world order of the US, other orderly countries and general chaos; the rebirth of religion as a political force; and the importance of science and technology in solving our problems, economic and environmental alike.

- *20:21 Vision* by Bill Emmott, published by Penguin Allen Lane. The editor of *The Economist* reckons that only two questions really matter when we are thinking about our future in the twenty-first century. One is whether capitalism will survive, thrive and retain its current, unusual allegiance around the world. The other is whether the United States of America will continue to maintain its dominance. Were this not to be the case, says Emmott, we'll all be rooned.

- *A Terrible Beauty* by Peter Watson, published by Phoenix Press. Almost 800 pages long, a ludicrously ambitious attempt to trace the history of all the big ideas of the twentieth century and how they influence us today. Great to dip into if you want to know what Freud or Adorno or Picasso or Foucault was on about.

- *On Equilibrium* by John Ralston Saul. The Canadian philosopher writer looks at the human condition in its modern context, and comes to the conclusion that we are all out of balance. To get back into kilter we need to integrate six qualities into our normal life: common sense, ethics, imagination, intuition, memory and reason.

Websites, just a few . . .

www.opendemocracy.co.uk—a media commentator's dream site, with informed articles by intelligent people on everything in this book and more.

www.whitehouse.org—simply hilarious. Buy the t-shirts.

www1.worldbank.org/economicpolicy/globalization/—the World Bank's take on the globalisation debate.

www.worldbank.org/poverty—resources and information for people working to understand and alleviate poverty.

http://www.globalenvision.org/—how the free marketers see poverty reduction.

www.un.org/popin—the UN's population website.

www.tai.org.au—home page of the Australia Institute.

Intro

Bobby Kennedy's speech: http://www.jfklibrary.org/r060 666a.htm

Money and work

Richard Franks, *Luxury Fever: Why Money Fails to Satisfy in an Era of Excess*, The Free Press, 1999. An analysis of the great twenty-first century rich-world disease: affluenza.

Clive Hamilton, *Growth Fetish*, Allen & Unwin, Sydney, 2003. Let's all just consume a little less frantically, shall we?

Paul Krugman, *The Return of Depression Economics*, Penguin Allen Lane, London, 1999. The global economy, the emerging market crises, and how it may all go wrong again.

David Landes, *The Wealth and Poverty of Nations: Why Some Are So Rich and Some So Poor*, W.W. Norton & Company, London, 1999. Update on Montaigne's ideas about why temperate climates breed economic success. No remarks on the economic revolution heralded by air conditioning.

Lord Richard Layard, *Happiness—Has Social Science a Clue?*, Lionel Robbins Memorial Lectures 2003, Centre for Economic Performance, London School of Economics.

Kenneth Pomeranz, *The Great Divergence: China, Europe and the Making of the Modern World Economy (The Princeton Economic*

History of the Western World), 2002. We took the high road etc.

Simon Schama, *The Embarrassment of Riches: Interpretation of Dutch Culture in the Golden Age*, London, 1988. Too many toys now, too many Vermeers then. How the Dutch spent their money.

Environment

Robin Baker, *Fragile Science*, Macmillan, London, 2001. Includes a great, if sceptical, exposition of the science of global warming, and looks at the question of whether sunscreen is more likely to give you skin cancer than the sun.

Jesse L. Byock, *Viking Age Iceland*, Penguin 2001. Fascinating account of the people who invented the modern novel, among other things.

Rachel Carson, *Silent Spring*, Houghton & Mifflin, New York, 2002. Fertiliser and pesticides, killing the birds! First written in 1963. The original pollution shocker.

Tim Flannery, *Quarterly Essay 9: Beautiful Lies*, Black Inc. 2003. All about salinity and the lies we use to justify the environmental holocaust in Australia.

Nigel Nicholson, *Managing the Human Animal*, Texere, London, 2000. It's nature, not nurture—get it?

David Suzuki and Holly Dressel, *Good News for a Change: Hope for a Troubled Planet*, Greystone Books, New York, 2003. Do it sustainably.

This article in *International Herald Tribune*, 20 January 2003 marked the publication of an IGBP book, *Global Change and the Earth System: A Planet Under Pressure*, by Margot Wallstrom, the European environment commissioner; Professor Bert Bolin, founding chair of the Intergovernmental Panel on Climate Change; Professor Paul Crutzen, winner of the 1995 Nobel Prize for chemistry; and Dr Will Steffen, director of the International Geosphere-Biosphere Programme (IGBP).

Science

John Seeley Brown and Paul Duguid, *The Social Life of Information*, Harvard Business School Press, Boston, 2000. Two techies take technology to task.

Gregg Herken, *Brotherhood of the Bomb: The Tangled Lives and Loyalties of Robert Oppenheimer, Ernest Lawrence and Edward Teller*, Henry Holt Books, New York, 2002. Gossipy account of three of the greatest scientists of the twentieth century.

Ray Kurtzweil, *The Age of Spiritual Machines*, Viking Penguin, New York, 1999. The development of artificial intelligence, and where we're all going with it.

Hans Morevic, *Robot: Mere Machine to Transcendent Mind*, Oxford University Press, Oxford, 1999. Science fiction without the fiction.

Roy Porter, *The Greatest Benefit to Mankind: A Medical History of Humanity*, W.W. Norton & Company, 1999. A reminder of mankind's great lack of progress in medical history.

Martin Rees, *Our Final Hour: A Scientist's Warning: How Terror, Error, and Environmental Disaster Threaten Humankind's Future In This Century—On Earth and Beyond*, Basic Books, London, 2003. Mad, self-replicating robots and nuclear accidents.

www.tranhumanism.org—where those who concern themselves with this stuff meet.

Democracy

Alexis de Tocqueville, *Democracy in America*, Everyman's Library, New York, 1994. Frenchman wanders through the states a couple of hundred years ago.

John Dewey, *Democracy and Education*, The Macmillan Company, 1916.

Francis Fukuyama, *The End of History and the Last Man*, Free Press, 1992.—See page 98–9 for this book's main thesis.

UN Human Development Report 2002, *Deepening Democracy in a Fragmented World*, UNDP. Facts, figures, why it's good, why it's bad, everything you could ever want to know about the state of democracy on the earth.

Security

Andrew Bacevik, *American Empire: The Realities and Consequences of US Diplomacy*, Harvard University Press, Boston 2002.

Zbiegniew Brzezinski, *The Grand Chessboard: American Primacy and its Geostrategic Imperatives*, Basic Books, 1997. So what's going on in Eurasia, then?

Samuel P. Huntington, *Why International Primacy Matters*, International Security, Spring 1993. The original essay which led to the book.

——*The Clash of Civilisations and the Remaking of World Order*, Touchstone Books, New York, 1998. Why the Arab world and the west is going to fight and keep on fighting.

Michael Moore, *Stupid White Men . . . and other Sorry Excuses for the State of the Nation*, Regan Books, New York, 2002. American slob lets loose on the new rulers of the world.

——*Dude, Where's My Country?*, Warner Books, New York, 2003. As above.

John Pilger, *The New Rulers of the World*, Verso, 2002. The case against the American Empire by the quintessential 1970s lefty journalist in a white suit.

People, people, people . . .

Paul Ehrlich, *The Population Bomb*, Amerion, New York, 1976. We're all going to die!

Garrett Hardin, *The Ostrich Factor: Our Population Myopia*, Oxford University Press, New York, 1999. As above.

Paul Hawken, *The Ecology of Commerce*, Harper Collins, New York, 1993. People are breeding exponentially.

Massimo Livi-Bacci, *A Concise History of World Population*, Blackwell, London, 1997. Does what it says on the box.

Dennis L. Meadows et al., *The Limits to Growth*, Universe Books, New York, 1972. Hey, we're running out of stuff.

——*Beyond the Limits*, Earthscan, New York, 1992. We really are running out of stuff.

Frances Moore Lapp and Rachel Schurman, *Taking Population Seriously*, Earthscan, New York, 1992.

Julian Simon, *The Ultimate Resource 2*, Princeton, 1996. We're right as rain.

Igjo Tydings, *Born to Starve*, UNRISD, New York, 1975. Gloom and doom.

Corporate power

Peter Cain and Tony Hopkins, *British Imperialism 1688–2000*, Longman, London, 2001. Finance and fighting—the money that drove the empire.

Niall Ferguson, *Empire*, Penguin Allen Lane, London, 2003. For background on one of the greater multinationals in history, Britain. America: shoulder the burden, says Ferguson.

Thomas Frank, *One Market Under God: Extreme Capitalism, Market Populism and the End of Democracy*, Secker & Warburg, New York, 2001. The case for the prosecution.

Noreena Hertz, *The Silent Takeover: Global Capitalism and the Death of Democracy*, Arrow, London, 2001. How television is destroying Bhutan and other tales from the global economy.

Naomi Klein, *No Logo*, Flamingo, London, 2001. Totally unbranded publishing phenomenon.

Philip Lawson, *The East India Company: A History*, Longman Publishing Group, New York, 1995. Worthy trawl through the centuries with the original corporate buccaneers.

John Micklethwait and Adrian Wooldridge, *The Company: A Short History of a Revolutionary Idea*, Modern Library, 2003. A romp through the entertaining world of the joint stock company.

George Monbiot, *Captive State: The Corporate Takeover of Britain*, Pan Books, London, 2001. The global justice movement's mouthpiece on how corporations are destroying our lives.

Tom Peters and Robert Waterman, *In Search of Excellence*, Warner Books, 1982. From the original management gurus, a selection of excellent companies, many of which subsequently disappeared.

Globalisation

Richard Fletcher, *The Conversion of Europe*, HarperCollins, New York, 1997. How Christianity came to dominate the continent, but much more besides.

Thomas L. Freidman, *The Lexus and the Olive Tree*, Anchor, New York, 2000. Classic on globalisation from a *New York Times* columnist.

Douglas Irwin, *Free Trade Under Fire*, Princeton University Press, Princeton, 2003. It's the least bad system says Professor Irwin, a model of reasonableness.

Paul Kennedy, *The Rise & Fall of British Naval Mastery*, Krieger Publishing Company, London, 1982. The importance of gunboats in persuading people to do business with you.

Paul Krugman, *Crises: The Price of Globalization?*, August 2000. Paper presented to the Jackson Hole Symposium.

Angus Maddison, *The World Economy: A Millennium Perspective*, OECD, 2001. A thousand years of history in a book with a lousy cover.

Jerry Mander and Edward Goldsmith, *The Case Against the Global Economy*, Sierra Club Books, San Francisco, 1996. The lefties from the International Forum on Globalisation collect together essays from the global justice movement's lead spokespeople.

Donald Moggeridge, et al., eds, *The Collected Writings of John Maynard Keynes, vol. 21: National Self Sufficiency*, Macmillan and Cambridge University, London, 1978.

George Monbiot, *The Age of Consent: A Manifesto for a New World Order*, Flamingo, London, 2003. Tear it all down and build it up different.

Kevin O'Rourke and Jeffrey Williamson, *Globalization and History: The Evolution of a Nineteenth-century Atlantic Economy*, MIT Press, Boston, 2001. Globalisation? We've been here before and it all went badly wrong in the Wall Street crash.

Anita Roddick, *Take it Personally: How Globalisation Affects You and How to Fight Back*, HarperCollins, New York, 2001. Colourful exposition of anti-globalisation arguments by Body Shop founder and friends.

Robert Skidelsky, *John Maynard Keynes: Fighting for Britain 1937–1946*, Macmillan, London, 2001. All about those hilarious Bretton Woods negotiations, and anything else you wanted to know about JMK, in the third of a three volume biography.

Joseph Stiglitz, *Globalisation and its Discontents*, Penguin Allen Lane, London, 2002. Nobel laureate, formerly chief economist at the World Bank says what's wrong with the IMF.

Armand Van Dormael, *Bretton Woods: The Birth of a Monetary System*, Holmes & Meier Publishers, Inc., New York, 1978. Everything you ever wanted to know about how the ugly sisters of Washington came into being.

Conclusion

Manuel Castells, *The Rise of the Network Society*, Blackwell Publishers, London, 2000. We're all connected, man.

Alvin Toffler, *The Third Wave*, William Collins Sons & Co. Ltd., New York, 1980. The original futurologist foresees big changes.

INDEX